The Truth About Money

What Schools Don't Teach About Capitalism

TIMSIMON "BAMBOO" KIMANI

The Truth About Money

Printed in the United States of America.

Paperback ISBN:

Ebook ISBN:

Editor: Pamela Brinkley

www.thepaperpulpit.com

Published by Erica Mukisa and Timsimon Kimani

Email: info@lifeisspiritual.org +25 471 706 2098 +25 479 973 3775

Life is Spiritual Ministries

P.O. Box 1929 - 00232

Ruiru, Kenya, East Africa

Acknowledgements

For those of you who may not know who I am, I will simply begin by introducing myself. My name is Timsimon Kuria Kimani. I was born in Kenya, but grew up and was educated in the United States of America. I grew up in California but traveled to Kenya in my early teenage years to live with my uncle George Macharia, his wife Mary and his children (my cousins) Levi Kuria, Edith N., Asnath W. and James Sheve Macharia.

These early years with my cousins did a lot to help shape who I became. I will forever be indebted and grateful to them. By the time I left the U.S. for Kenya as a teenager I had no idea of my identity, my heritage, the meaning of my name, my background, and who my people were, etc. I would also like to acknowledge Pastor Mrs. Fanny Mrima who played a key role in my upbringing during my last year of high school. She brought me into her home and provided a beautiful, godly atmosphere for me to study hard for my exams. I will forever be grateful to her and her five children (now grown) Joel, Jimmy, Joy, Joses and Jerry. During these years while my parents were in the United States, it would have been impossible for me to do as well as I did in High School. I would also like to thank my parents, who raised me in a Christian home and instilled the mentality of wisdom into me at an early age. Thank you, Mom and Dad, may God richly bless you!

Introduction

Traveling gave me a great deal of wisdom and helped to open my eyes as to who I am. Growing up in America (while coming from another country) can cause one to be unaware of one's identity. That is one of the key things I share in this book because identity is part of purpose and purpose plays a key role in making and earning money. If you earn money through your purpose, then money works for you. If you earn money through employment, then you work for money. I finished high school and went straight into music. Years later, my music took off, and I became a household name in Kenya. My fans knew me as "Bamboo African Bantu," but God had an entirely different plan for my life outside of secular hip hop music and entertainment. I interned at Universal Records in New York City, their marketing department was and is very aggressive. I wrote music for Konvict Muzik (Akon's record label) a record label in Atlanta, Georgia for a very short time but while I was there I learned a lot. After giving my life to Christ, I came into one of the toughest seasons in my life. If you can't make money in the clubs or promote any of the "worldly" products and events like alcohol or festivals for which you used to before salvation, how does one cross over and still make a living? Especially if you're in a 3rd world country. In America, it is a little easier to get a job than it is in Africa.

Very many secular artists want to give their lives to Christ, but wonder how they will make the transition and still feed their families. Many times Christians have no idea what to tell them because many Christians themselves are in financial hardship. "Trust in the Lord," they say, or "God will make a way." These promises sound great, but I needed rent money now! These times can be the most difficult and frustrating. I have also written this book to encourage you. Times will get better. God has not abandoned you. This time of training will build you up and strengthen you to build others. Your personal leadership is being formed in the furnace of affliction, self-determination is built into you as so-called "friends" abandon you, and you are left to figure things out on your own.

Life's greatest lessons are learned in this stage of life. God allows the pain because He can see the strength of wisdom being forged into your spirit. In this stage of life you may reflect extensively, feel isolated, humbled, ~~one~~ learns how to pray - but praying for money all the time is not sustainable. I'm not saying that God does not give His children money, He does. However, God wants to train managers and this is man's main job in life. Management is the effective, efficient, correct and timely use of another person's property and resources for the purpose for which they were delegated with a view to producing the expected added value to the person. To clarify, management implies that it should be better when it returns. God will give you what you can manage. God wants you to be an economist.

Being an economist simply means getting the most out of the least, or getting the maximum out of the minimum. Myles Munroe said, "Answered prayer is regulated by your capacity to manage. Anything you fail to manage, you will lose." In hindsight, one can imagine all the mismanagement which resulted in catastrophic losses.

> *"Blessed are the meek, for they shall inherit the earth." (Matthew 5:5)*

Meek means self-discipline. The idea is that those with self-discipline and management skills will end up owning the property. Hollywood movies and modern-day music videos with deceitful visuals of easy success and quick overnight riches do our youth a huge disservice. The quick path to riches is a shortcut to hell.

"Like a partridge that hatches eggs it did not lay, are those who gain riches by unjust means.

> *When their lives are half gone, their riches will desert them, and in the end they will prove to be fools." (Jeremiah 17:11 NIV)*

What we are dealing with when it comes to finances is a real life monopoly game where few have been given capital to begin with while the rest have to start from scratch. For those who do not know what the game of monopoly is, I'll briefly explain. Monopoly is a board game which reflects the real life game of capitalism. In this game, players roll the dice (representing chance) and move around the board buying and trading properties and developing them into hotels and homes. Then one player can collect rents from their opponents who are the other players also moving around the board. The difference is that at the beginning of the game, each player is given $1,500 USD capital (board game money) to start with. One must then be careful how one moves in the game because it is possible to land in jail with a roll of the dice or end up in someone's hotel or property where you are forced to pay for accommodation. The goal is to end up with as much property as possible and force the others into bankruptcy.

We as human beings are in a real life monopoly game, but the problem is that the vast majority of us have not been given capital to start with and are therefore forced to start from scratch. We find ourselves in other people's properties, and we are forced to pay money we don't have or the ability to access. As if that is not enough, if one is poor, he is ridiculed and despised for it, excluded from acquiring knowledge and skills (lacking money to pay for school fees) and relegated to the bottom of the social, political and economic totem pole. There are few stories of those who rise from rags to riches but for the vast majority, this dream seems to be nothing more than just that, a dream. Then as the sun rises, they wake up to yet another economic nightmare. The process begins from childhood where one is forced to pay for school fees. If the parents of the child do not have money, they are excluded from having access to knowledge. The knowledge they need so that they can eventually get a job and work for money. This situation is looked into further in later chapters of this publication, however, charging a child for knowledge is inherently wrong and any nation that participates in it is doing their youth a disservice. Nobody is born with money, and excluding those who have no money from having access to knowledge is evil on primary and secondary levels.

During the colonial era, the British government offered her citizens vast stretches of prime farmland in British colonies like Kenya and Uganda and South Africa. These were loans given to British citizens which were to be repaid to the British government over time. The British government did for her citizens what every competent government should do for their citizens. Offer startup loans to give your citizens a fighting chance at the game of monopoly. Many British citizens became rich because of this opportunity to create wealth at the expense of Africans who were herded into small overcrowded infertile lands to fend for themselves. Poor Africans were excluded from the monopoly game from the very beginning. By the time independence from Great Britain was declared on December 12th, 1963, vast quantities of the most prime land were already in the hands of a few prominent families like the Kenyattas. To make matters worse, the British farmers who left were compensated for their farms in full, but the Africans from whom the farms had been stolen were never compensated.

H.E. Jomo Kenyatta had promised Kenyans that he would restore lands stolen from them by the British to the victimized communities. Instead, he amassed vast quantities of Kenya's most prime real estate for himself, his family and his colleagues. The seeds of corruption were planted by the British colonial authorities, the harvest of hardship and inequality was left for Africans to reap. For more on this topic, please read: "Kenya Looters and Grabbers 54 Years of Corruption and Plunder by the Elite, 1963 - 2017" by Joe Khamisi. In chapter five he writes, "Kenyatta, for one, went on an acquisition binge, obtaining everything he could find for himself and his family - from cars to real estate. Moreover, he did not restrain officials in government from engaging in illegal activities and in amassing wealth without minding laws. It was like a contagious disease.

It engulfed everyone at the top of the public sector, leaving in its wake impunity and a feeling of hopelessness on the part of the rest of Kenyans." The exclusion from economic participation had commenced from those early days. The elite had distributed startup capital among themselves, everyone else was left to start from scratch.

The United States government is no stranger to the monopoly game of exclusion. The U.S. government had promised 40 acres and a mule to black Hebrew farmers. (Forty acres and a mule is part of Special Field Orders Number 15, it was a promise made by the United States government for agricultural reform to aid formerly enslaved black farmers.) Needless to say, the former slave farmers were never given any land or animals and were instead relegated to the bottom of the social, political and economic sectors of human existence. This knowledge is not designed to discourage you, but rather to give you a realistic overview of the world in which we live and to offer you a point of reference from where to begin your journey for financial freedom. All is not lost. I am in no way giving anyone an excuse to give up and not try to make progress in life. If anything, God's word is clear on this topic.

> *"Lazy hands make a man poor, but a diligent hand brings wealth." (Proverbs 10:4)*

Furthermore, the whole earth belongs to our Heavenly Father.

> *"The earth is the LORD's, and everything in it, the world, and all who live in it;" (Psalms 24:1)*

Currently, with technology and all the wealth that can be created through it, the playing field has in no way been made equal but new opportunities have been made available. Opportunities are open for all to take advantage of. We can become wealthy as our minds grow and gain a more in-depth understanding of management. Hedge fund managers manage some of the largest money pools in the world. One's ability to manage resources well will result in the accumulation and acquisition of more resources.

Hard times will show whether you were a good manager or a bad manager. True maturity is the proper management of all that God has given you. For most of us who did not have access to free money (start- up capital) in the forms of a large inheritance or lottery winnings or any other financial windfall, money is the outcome of giving massive value and applying correct business principles. Some people believe that the only people who do not make money by earning it are politicians. This as you will see in further chapters is just a small part of our flawed system called capitalism. We are compelled to prefer capitalism because the alternative (communism and/or socialism) is even worse. Anyone who does not gain the rule over money and learn to control it, will inevitably end up with it controlling you. Gaining control over money requires great maturity, if there is no maturity, you remain a child and a child is not fit to rule.

> *"Now I say, as long as the heir is a child, he does not differ at all from a slave, although he is owner of everything, but he is under guardians and managers until the date set by the father. So, also we, while we were children, were held in bondage under the elemental things of the world." (Galatians 4:1-3 NASV)*

God gives his toughest assignments to His strongest soldiers. Out of these tough and painful times come precious stones of wisdom which are designed to uplift and strengthen you so that you can turn around and help others and help the lost cross over to the Kingdom of God. One disadvantage of Satan's kingdom which works in our favor is that it excludes the vast majority of the world's citizens. That opens the doors for Christians to educate and raise up as many of them as possible to rebel against the god of this world and serve the Lord Jesus Christ. If you've not been under pressure, it means there were no diamonds being formed in you. This time of transition is a time I also passed through.

Some people take many weeks, others take months, mine took years. Through those years, I traveled back to the United States, spent years studying and getting a first world education, after which I came back to Kenya. I had been gone for seven years. I studied political science, history, theology and spent time in the music industry learning the ins and outs of the most influential entertainment industry in the world, the American entertainment industry. Furthermore, I found out that Satan owns and controls the American entertainment industry (and not just the entertainment industry, but this whole world (2 Corinthians 4:4). Satan controls Hollywood, and many internationally known celebrity actors and actresses are satanists behind the scenes. They sell their souls for money, power and fame. The irony is that by training your mind through the appropriate disciplines, they could have even more success through fulfillment of purpose than whatever success they think they have now after compromising their integrity. Selling your soul is a compromise of integrity. Any building whose structural integrity has been compromised will eventually be condemned and brought down. A life is built like a well- structured building, from the foundation to the rooftop. Success through compromise of integrity is short-lived success.

It does not last long, especially since that which you

compromise to obtain, you must compromise to keep. Many celebrities are drug and/or alcohol addicts behind the scenes. The drugs help them temporarily silence their conscience because wrongdoing brings shame and regret. Their fans have no idea what is happening, but they find themselves emulating their favorite celebrities. As soon as they do that, they're under that celebrity's spell. They become fanatical. Whatever bad habit their favorite celebrity has is what they repeat in their lifestyle. In so doing, they delve into a lifestyle of deeper sin. Sin soon brings death, which is what Satan and his agents want. The industry is not about money power and fame; those are just tools which Satan uses to pull millions of souls to hell. Satan's agents are in bondage. His system is a system of bondage. Many Christians came from the world and tried to cross over into Christianity but because of lack of finances, they got sucked back into the world.

Financial freedom can ease the suffering of millions of families around the world and help to make this world a better place for all. Financial education and financial intelligence can help deliver those who are in bondage to Satan because of lack of finances. No prostitute in their right mind would sell themselves if they were financially stable. People are generally less likely to steal or compromise their integrity if they have everything they need. This book was written to help people who are wondering why the area of finances seems to be so confusing and frustrating. Having information can give someone an added advantage in life. If you were financially stable, it would be difficult for Satan to persuade you to compromise for money. If Satan has no in-roads to your life, he will leave you for a season and go for the "low-hanging fruit," Christians. Being financially stable takes work. It takes knowledge and it takes wisdom. For those who are willing to pay the price, there is a great reward. The best part of financial freedom is that you get to be generous with your money. You can help out so many desperate people and be someone's answer to prayer. God can use you to uplift the standard of living of an entire nation. The best part is that every act of kindness you perform is documented in Heaven and there is a return on that investment in eternity. Without financial education and financial understanding as part of the core educational curriculum, schools do a huge disservice to our children, our country, and the world, failing to prepare them for the real world. By failing to teach in detail about money and to emphasize on financial intelligence in school, the system creates adults who are unprepared for the real world. The vast majority of adults in the world have next to no financial education, despite having degrees and PhDs in all kinds of academic fields. Many college and university professors can barely pay their bills. They are stuck in the ruthless financial rat- race, which prevents them from ever moving forward or excelling into the ever elusive world of financial freedom. Their salaries are heavily taxed and then deductions are made to contribute to their pensions in retirement, but even those pensions or retirement plans are heavily taxed, and that is if they even receive their pension payments after retirement at all.

Instead of guiding students into the light of financial freedom, our education system is leading millions of young people into financial darkness and the worst kind of debt: Student loan debt. In the United States, student loan debt is over $1.2 trillion USD. In the criminal world, this is called extortion. If American students are being plundered by the educational system, one can only imagine the extent of the plunder in Africa. In Africa, children are charged for primary (elementary school) and secondary (high school) education. Although there are some African countries where primary school education is paid for by the government, these public schools are often overcrowded and understaffed and the staff themselves are underpaid. This makes it almost impossible for the poor to access quality education. Charging a child for education or knowledge is fundamentally wrong. It is actually evil. Look at it like this, if one must have money to pay school fees, and then to have money one must have a job, and then to have a job one must have an education, and to have an education, one must pay school fees, the odds are already stacked against the child.

Who in the world was born with money? You may say that the child's parents should pay for the child, but this system started at some point with some people already being excluded from having access to knowledge for lack of money. This exclusion from knowledge is evil, and should be fought against by good people. These are some of the shortcomings of Capitalism. There are hardly any people in the world who would not like to be rich.

> *This should tell you that the vast majority of humanity desires wealth, and rightfully so. Wealth offers financial freedom and power, and deep down inside the heart of all of humanity there is an innate desire for power. Nobody wants to be a slave. Yet, the vast majority of employees are exactly that, slaves. They hate their jobs, but they are forced to work there because they need the salary to pay their bills. The job provides financial security. Financial security may sound good when compared to poverty, but there is another option which most people never have access to. That option is financial freedom. The truth is that financial security (provided by employment) is not far from maximum security provided by the prison system. Yes, financial security (slavery) and*

maximum security (prison) are next door neighbors. I am not condemning work, on the contrary, man cannot enjoy fulfillment in life without work. True work is the fulfillment of purpose. When an eagle is flying it is working, when a fish is swimming, it is working, even though it cannot see the water in which it swims. A cheetah pursuing a gazelle at a speed of over 80mph is working. The problem with most employment is that the job has nothing to do with the fulfillment of the employee's purpose, which causes a feeling of hopelessness and powerlessness. This is part of the reason Jesus says in Matthew 11:28-30:

"Come unto me, all ye that labor and are heavy laden, and I will give you rest. Take my yoke upon you, and learn of me; for I am meek and lowly in heart: and ye shall find rest unto your souls. 30 For my yoke is easy, and my burden is light."

Jesus is reaching out to the slaves, the oppressed, those who live in sin, those who are forced into a life they did not choose, those who feel they have no way out. Those who are like fish out of water, those eagles whose wings have been clipped, those cheetahs whose legs are tied and have no speed. Jesus is offering them their true identities, their true purpose. This is why he says, "I will give you rest." because when one finds his/her true purpose and discovers their God- given identity, they begin to swim through life, they find it easier to hunt.

They are more fulfilled because they are pursuing their purpose and fulfilling their destiny, they're full of life! They are happier and this happiness can be seen by others who desire this same happiness. This is how true Christianity is spread.

> *"For my yoke is easy, and my burden is light." (Matthew 11:30)*

A "yoke" is defined as - a wooden cross piece that is fastened over the necks of two animals and attached to the plow or cart that they are to pull. The synonyms (words that mean the same thing or have similar meanings) of yoke include a harness, or collar. In other words, Jesus is saying that his way of life is purposeful and far more fulfilling. "Light" in this verse also connotes knowledge. So, he is telling us that his way of life is purposeful, fulfilling and enlightening or filled with knowledge. Knowledge which can help make life far better for everyone. There are only two kinds of "yokes" in the world, Satan's yoke and Jesus' yoke. All human beings are under one of these two yokes. One is light (knowledge, wisdom, life) the other is darkness (ignorance, false knowledge, vanity, foolishness, death). It is up to you to choose which yoke best fits you.

> *"An hypocrite with his mouth destroys his neighbor: but through knowledge shall the just be delivered." (Proverbs 11:9)*

Without knowledge, humanity has no chance at a purpose filled life.

> *"My people are destroyed for lack of knowledge: because thou hast rejected knowledge, I will also reject thee, that thou shalt be no priest to me: seeing thou hast forgotten the law of thy God, I will also forget thy children." (Hosea 4:6)*

If children have no access to quality education, another generation of godlessness can be expected. If children are prevented from accessing knowledge because of their poverty and inability to pay school fees, then another generational cycle of poverty and hopelessness has been projected into society. A cycle of darkness which can only be stopped by a great light. The light of the knowledge of the truth.

> *"And you will know the truth, and the truth will make you free." (John 8:32)-Jesus Christ AD 33*

The truth is that the educational system, not just in Africa but around the world (in America as well) has not provided the kind of education students need to survive and thrive in today's global economy. There are two areas of management a human being must have to live well on the earth and make it to Heaven after your time here is done.

1. The management of your relationship with God and,

2. The management of your relationship with Money.

"And Jesus answering said unto them, render to Caesar the things that are Caesar's, and to God the things that are God's." (Mark 12:17)

Every human being must learn to manage these two relationships; their relationship with God and their relationship with money. If you can perfect these two, you are well on your way to Heaven and should be teaching others to do the same. If your relationship with God is intact, then your relationship with your fellow man will be in order as well, since God has commanded that we love one another. You cannot have a strong relationship with God and simultaneously be mistreating your spouse, children or fellow man. A strong relationship with God will solidify your relationship with your fellow man. A relationship with God is strengthened by learning of Him through His word. The more of His word you know, the more you know of Him. Simple.

Your relationship with money is next on the list as the second most important relationship you must learn to manage. If one compromises their integrity to obtain money, their relationship with God will be tarnished.

> *"For the love of money is a root of all sorts of evil, and some by longing for it have wandered away from the faith and pierced themselves with many griefs." (1Timothy 6:10)*

(New American Standard Bible)

Many people believe that money is the root of all evil. That is NOT true and that is NOT what the Bible says. It says that "the LOVE OF MONEY is the root of all evil.". In other words, the insatiable desire for money to the extent that one is willing to compromise one's integrity to obtain it, is a way to allow all kinds of evil to enter into the world. On the other hand, if you have a healthy relationship with money, the result is financial freedom, and it is possible to have this while still living a righteous life.

> *"But seek ye first the Kingdom of God and his righteousness and all these things shall be added unto you." (Matthew 6:33)*

> *"Wealth and riches shall be in his house, and his righteousness endures forever. Unto the upright*

there arises light in the darkness, he is gracious and full of compassion and righteous." (Psalms 112:3,4)

Psalms 112 talks about wealth, riches and righteousness in one verse. Verse four says that "unto the upright there arises light in the darkness.".

This "light" is knowledge. This knowledge is what the prince of this world does not want you to have. Satan is the prince of this world.

"In whom the god of this world has blinded the minds of them which believe not, lest the light of the glorious gospel of Christ, who is the image of God, should shine unto them."(2 Corinthians 4:4)

Satan (the god of this world, whose name means adversary) is blinding the minds of humanity. How is he doing this? Through education. His satanic form of useless education. By filling the minds of students with useless information which they will never use in real life situations and then examining them on this same useless information and giving them a pass or fail mark thereby telling them that they are either failures in life if they fail the exam or that they are winners in life if they pass the exam. But being able to remember useless information does not qualify one for success in life. I remember being taught the various parts of a fly in high school. I could tell you about a compound eye, but I could not cook for myself or tell you about the most nutritious foods. Furthermore, I could not present a financial statement, which is what a banker looks at, not your school, leaving certificate or your grades. No banker cares if you graduated first in your class. No lending institution cares what school you went to. The bank manager wants to know if you understand money. Do you have financial intelligence? I'm sure you can remember some useless things you learned in school which will never help you in real life situations. Why are schools filling us with useless information?

Part of the aim of writing this book is to answer that question and help readers manage the relationships which really matter in life. First their relationship with God, this is learned through prayer and reading your bible regularly and understanding what is being said, if you don't understand, seek further knowledge. There are plenty of authors who have written books about this area. I suggest you read everything Myles Munroe has written. There are few authors I look up to, but he is definitely one of them. If you desire to grow quickly in Christianity, I suggest you read and grow in knowledge. Feed your mind, and the rest will follow.

The focus of this book, however, is the second relationship which must be managed, your relationship with money. Mismanaging your relationship with money can destroy your relationship with God.

Many men and women of God started well in ministry, but because of a lack of financial intelligence, coupled with a lack of integrity they eventually compromised, because of lack of money. In all honesty, the lack of money can be a root of evil. No prostitute would be standing on the corner in the middle of the night in the cold if they were rich or even financially stable. Indeed, capitalism has sent many to hell, but the alternative (communism and socialism) have sent even more.

> *"The rich man's wealth is his strong city; the destruction of the poor is their poverty."(Proverbs 10:15)*

Poverty and destruction go hand in hand. Where there is poverty, there is destruction.

> *"The thief comes not, but for to steal and to kill and to destroy: I am come that they might have life and that they might have it more abundantly." (John 10:10)*

Wherever you see destruction of human life, you know the thief, the adversary, the devil has been at work, doing what he does best. Making industries out of human suffering. Satan, the prince of darkness, is the prince of ignorance. He can only rule over those who lack knowledge of God's word.

Wherever there is knowledge there is light, if your heart and mind are full of light, he cannot deceive you and if he cannot deceive you, he cannot destroy you. By maintaining a state of ignorance, poverty and desperation over the masses, Satan can maintain his dominion. But if the knowledge of the light of truth is spread, his kingdom will reduce in size until it is finally destroyed from the earth altogether. Jesus came to give us that knowledge of truth, that inside information that very few have, that knowledge I call, dangerous truth.

This book is here to deliver this dangerous truth and solve the problem of the lack of financial intelligence, financial wisdom and financial knowledge. If one cannot be corrupted, his relationship with God has a stronger chance of standing the test of time. May this book help you to be incorruptible.

Table of Contents

Chapter One

How It Began

> "It is well enough that people of the nation do not understand our banking and monetary systems, for if they did, I believe there would be a revolution before tomorrow morning."- Henry Ford

"Money does not grow on trees," is something my dad used to tell me. I suppose I always wondered where money came from. Nobody ever explained it to me. I had to search and research until I learned what many strangely have no idea about. Money does not come from the government. Most people think it does, but when it comes to money, most people are guessing through life. Thousands of students attend high school in order to learn how to go to institutions of higher learning such as universities and colleges, hoping to get a good job so that they can jump into the job market and find a great place to exchange their time for money. This is a common goal of the masses of graduates who emerge from institutions of higher learning. What a poor goal to have. So, why are we not educated as to where money comes from, and who issues it and how it is made and the factors affecting its production? Why is there no comprehensive in-depth study specifically on the subject of money?

Most people can tell that there's something not right with our money, but can't really put their finger on it and explain exactly what it is. Money is not a new concept, we find money spoken of in the bible when Abraham did business with Ephron in Genesis 23:16.

> "And Abraham hearkened unto Ephron; and Abraham weighed to Ephron the silver, which he had named in the audience of the sons of Heth, four hundred shekels of silver, current money with the merchant."

If we find money at the beginning of the bible, then it is definitely not a new concept. It has been in the world since the beginning. However, like everything else Satan finds that is pure, he makes a point of perverting. Money is no exception. The following is a brief history of how our modern-day currency came to be.

The year was 1694, England had just suffered through 50 years of war. With their funds exhausted, the English needed loans to fund their political ambitions.

A Scottish banker named William Paterson was one of the proponents of the privately owned central banking system.

But this malevolent system predates him. He was only one of the puppets to put forward that a privately owned bank which was to issue money to the government out of thin air was to be the solution. Of course, he did not put it in exactly those words. There is no way we can speak of modern-day money or banking as we know it without discussing a particular Jewish family, the house of Rothschild.

The Rothschilds have been controlling the world for a very long time. Their extended tentacles reach into many areas of our daily lives. The Rothschilds claim to be a Jewish family, but the truth is they are Khazars. The (so-called "Jews") originally came from a country called Khazaria, which is now mostly covered by Georgia (Eastern Europe). As later chapters in this publication will show, the Khazars, under instruction of the king, converted to Judaism in 740 AD. Their genes are however Asiatic Mongolian, but more on this in later chapters.

> "I know thy works, and tribulation and poverty, (but thou art rich) and I know the blasphemy of them which say they are Jews, and are not, but are the synagogue of Satan." (Revelation 2:9)

By far, the wealthiest bloodline in the world is never mentioned in any Forbes publication for obvious reasons, and the leader of the Ashkenazi Jews in the world today is the Rothschild family. Their bloodline also reaches into the royal families of Europe as well as the following family names: Astor, Bundy, Collins, DuPont, Freedman, Kennedy, Morgan, Oppenheimer, Rockefeller, Sassoon, Schiff, Van Duyne and Taft. Please note that not everyone you see with the above names are actually a part of these malevolent family Rothschild criminal networks. The majority of Ashkenazi Jews have nothing to do with this conspiracy and are just living their lives innocently. The intent of this chapter is not to single out a particular people for stigmatization, but rather to explain how we arrived at the current global economic situation we find ourselves in today.

In 1743, Mayer Amschel Bauer, an Ashkenazi Jew, was born in Frankfurt, Germany, the son of Moses Amschel Bauer, a moneylender. Moses Bauer places a red sign above the entrance to his counting house. This sign is a red hexagram (the geometric and numeric representation of 666) which under the dictates of the house of Rothschild will end up on the flag of Israel some two hundred years later.

(The six sided hexagram is not and has never been the "star of David," as most Christians naively believe. It is the star of Moloch found in Amos 5:26

> "But ye have borne the tabernacle of your Moloch and Chiun your images, the STAR of your god, which ye made to yourselves."

After the death of Amschel's father, he returned to Frankfurt to take over his father's business. Bauer changes his name to Rothschild (meaning Red shield) signifying the flag hanging over his door. The significance of this flag was so important to him that he changed his name to Rothschild in order to totally embody the spirit it represents.

In 1770 Mayer Amschel Rothschild drew up plans for the creation of the Illuminati and commissioned an Ashkenazi Jew, Adam Weishaupt, with its formation. The Illuminati was based upon the teachings of the Talmud, which is the oral tradition of the rabbinical Jews. The word "Illuminati" is a luciferian term meaning, keepers of the light.

Mayer had five sons (allegedly) and sent them to five European nations including England, Austria, France, Germany and Italy. Around 1790 Amschel Rothschild said something so significant it has been recorded in many historical accounts: "Permit me to issue and control the money of a nation, and I care not who makes its laws."

In 1791, the Rothschilds got control of America's money through Alexander Hamilton (their agent in George

Washington's cabinet) as they set up a central bank in the USA called the First Bank of the United States.

This was established with a 20-year charter. In 1798, a professor named John Robison of the University of Edinburgh, a leading intellect of his time, published a book entitled, "Proof of a Conspiracy Against All the Religions and Governments of Europe Carried on in the Secret Meetings of Freemasons, Illuminati and Reading Societies." This book gave details of the whole Rothschild Illuminati plan. Interestingly, in 1811 the charter for the Rothschild Bank of the United States ended and congress voted against renewing it. Nathan Mayer Rothschild is not amused and States categorically,

> "Either the application for renewal of the charter is granted, or the United States will find itself in a most disastrous war."

The US is not moved by the threats, and this causes Rothschild to issue another threat;

> "Teach those impudent Americans a lesson. Bring them back to colonial status."

Then, backed by Rothschild money and Nathan Mayer Rothschild's orders, the British declare war on the United States. The Rothschild's aim was to make the US build up so much debt in fighting the war, they would have no choice but to surrender to the Rothschilds and allow the charter for the Rothschild owned First Bank of the US to be renewed. This is the level of determination the house of Rothschild had concerning the planting of their own central banks in nations, and they will stop at nothing to establish that end. As of Wednesday, May 29, 2019, the only countries in the world without a Rothschild central bank are, North Korea, Iran, Sudan (recent changes in Sudan's political environment are changing with the ousting of Bashir), Afghanistan (although this nation may have succumbed to the pressure through U.S. invasion), Iraq (the US/Iraq war has since changed that and a Rothschild central bank has been established by conquest). Clearly, the nations in the world with the most "notoriety" as far as the mainstream media is concerned, are the nation's which still resist the establishment of Rothschild owned central banks. The system is clearly rigged. The invasion of Iraq, Afghanistan and the political unrest of nations such as Sudan has had nothing to do with the spread of democracy, but rather who gets to print the money. Their entire operations of global takeover are covered from public view by the mainstream media, which feeds the public with information of little to no real value.

Central banks are far more influential than laws, governments or politicians but because of the cooperation of the educational curriculum and the mainstream media, they are not the focus of the general public. By the 20th century, a group of bankers wanted to put a central bank in the United States of America. These men gathered off the coast of Jekyll Island and met for nine days, and there they wrote what was to become the Federal Reserve Act of 1913. This is documented and a matter of public record. Anyone can go and investigate this on their own, and I actually encourage you to do so.

Some of these men went on to write about these meetings in their personal biographies. Here is a quote from Frank Vanderlip, president of the National City Bank of New York dated February 9th 1935 in the Saturday evening post.

(Fair Use for purposes of education)

> "I was as secretive -indeed as furtive - as any conspirator. Discovery, we knew, simply must not happen, or else all our time and effort would be wasted. If it were to be exposed that our particular group had gotten together and written a banking bill, that bill would have no chance whatever of passage by congress. - Frank A. Vanderlip

The 6 men that Nelson Aldrich, a prominent American political figure and leader of the Republican Party in the US senate (where he served from 1881 to 1911), brought together included the heads of banks, branches of government such as the treasury and some of the richest people in earth at the time. To give you an idea of how rich they were, these six men represented a quarter of the world's wealth in 1910. The bankers told the American public that the purpose of the central bank was to stabilize the economy and to stop the growth of Wall Street banks' control over America. The problem was that the people who wrote the bill were the very same people they said would stop. The foxes were guarding the hen house. If they succeeded, it would give a small group of people the power to create money from nothing and lend it to the American government with interest. This was all done in secret because back then, unlike today, the American public knew what a central bank was and people did not want a central bank. They knew everywhere there was a central bank, there would be wealth inequality, wild swings between economic booms and busts, and after each bust, those at the top of society mysteriously came out richer while everyone else became poorer.

The Federal Reserve was originally drafted as the Aldrich bill. But when it came into congress, they recognized senator Aldrich's name and smelled a rat. The bankers needed a better cover. They decided to send two millionaire friends to carry the bill to quell the suspicions of congress, and renamed it the Federal Reserve Act.

Then, in a brilliantly deceitful manner, the bankers set out to fool the American people through disinformation. In the newspapers of the day, the bankers screamed and protested against the new Federal Reserve Bill. "It would ruin the banks." they exclaimed. The average person read the protest of the banks and thought, "if the banks are opposing it, it must be good for the people." Through this deception, they (the people) pushed the Federal Reserve Act through congress by force. The bankers also fooled congress by putting clauses in the bill that limited their power, only to remove them after the bill was passed. The double deception had the cunning, evil foresight of Satan himself. The bill was passed on December 23, 1913, while most of congress was out for the holidays and with that, a small group of men had a monopoly over the issuing and creation of American money.

(The Privately Owned Federal Reserve)

Today, the Federal Reserve is the most powerful entity in the United States. They are not ashamed to admit it, either.

> "The Federal Reserve is an independent agency and that means basically that there is no other agency of government that can overrule actions that we take. What the relationships are (between the U.S. government and the privately owned Federal Reserve) don't frankly matter."

-Former Chairman of the Federal Reserve Alan Greenspan

The Federal Reserve cannot even be touched by investigating bodies. This is relevant to people who are not

U.S. citizens because the central banking system from England and the United States has now been put into all countries and even consolidated power in parts of Europe as the European Central Bank (ECB).

(Post pic of European Central Bank logo here) (European Central Bank ECB)

African countries which were previously colonized by the west (e.g. Britain) also have central banks which allow the same global banking cartels to dominate and control the issuance of money. This unites the nations of the world under one economic policy.

(Central Bank of Kenya, a puppet branch of the global banking cartels)

The only countries in the world without central banks are North Korea, Iran and Cuba. In the year 2000, this list suspiciously included Afghanistan, Iraq and Libya. Since the end of World War 2, the U.S. dollar has been the reserve currency of the world. This means that all central banks hold U.S. dollars in their reserves. So, all other currencies are backed by the U.S. dollar. This means that your country is directly linked to the monetary policy in America.

Unfortunately, as we've already covered, in 1971 due to a falling U.S. dollar, international capital flows into gold, and the funding of the Vietnam War, former U.S. president Richard Nixon took the dollar off the gold standard. Ever since then, the dollar has been floating and backed by nothing.

(In 1971 Richard Nixon took the dollar off the gold standard, prior to this, gold stabilized the global economy)

(But after Nixon took the dollar off the gold standard, inflation began to rise and the value of the dollar began to decline)

So if the US dollar is backed by nothing, and other currencies are backed by the U.S. dollar, then all currencies are backed by nothing tangible but trust in the US government. This means that all currencies are "fiat currencies," and in Latin, "fiat" means "let it be done." The consequence of having money backed by nothing is that whenever the Federal Reserve creates money, it dilutes the currency supply of all other nations because their reserves are backed by the US Dollar. All those country's reserves are worth less each time money is created. In the past few years, the Federal Reserve has created trillions of dollars.

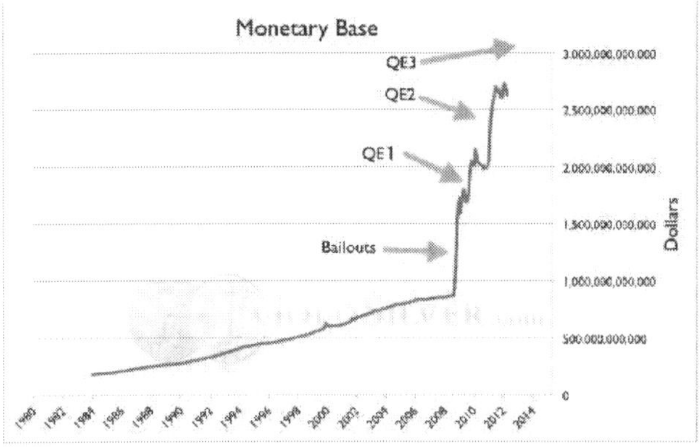

(QE Stands for Quantitative Easing which is an increase in the money supply, the bailouts of 2008 caused a sudden jump in the issuance of currency) Countries like China and Russia have noticed this. As a reaction to the money printing, these countries have been selling U.S. dollar reserves and buying gold over the same period to protect themselves against the coming downturn.

(Chinese President Xi Jinping and Russian President Vladimir Putin join forces to hold gold reserves instead of U.S. dollars)

The truth is that the whole economic system can run even though it is backed by nothing because of the people's faith. Faith that you can exchange your money for goods and services. Part of the reason for this faith is the fact that nobody really knows where money comes from. A Central Bank is basically an agency that manages a country's money supply. It loans money to the government with interest. Money which it has created out of thin air.

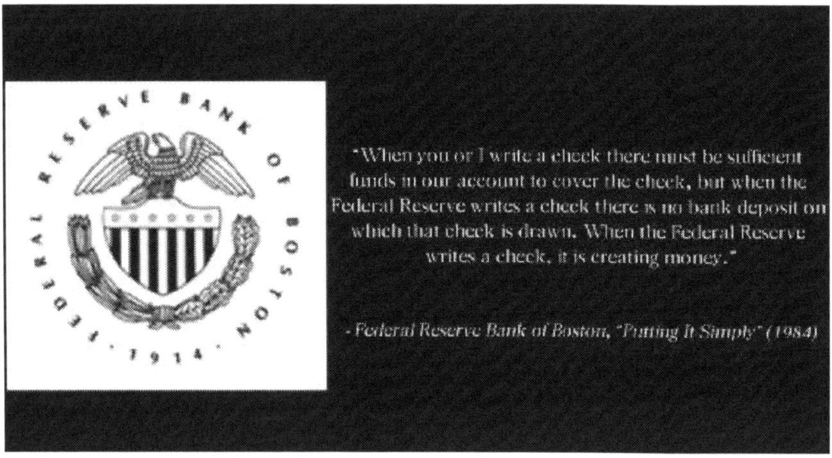

("When you or I write a check there must be sufficient funds in our account to cover the check, but when the Federal Reserve writes a check, there is no bank deposit on which that check is drawn. When the Federal Reserve writes a check, it's creating money." - Federal Reserve Bank of Boston, "Putting It Simply" (1984)

If you or I were to print our own currency, we would be put in jail for creating counterfeit money. But they can do it because they created the system.

Chapter Two

The Commercial Bank's Part of Money Creation

(Barclays, like other commercial banks, create money out of thin air every time you borrow money from them)

Every time you take out a loan to buy a house, a car, or a TV, banks create money out of nowhere to give you this money, and you still have to pay this money back with interest.

(As soon as your loan is approved, the bank creates the new money it lends to you out of thin air, this money must be repaid with interest)

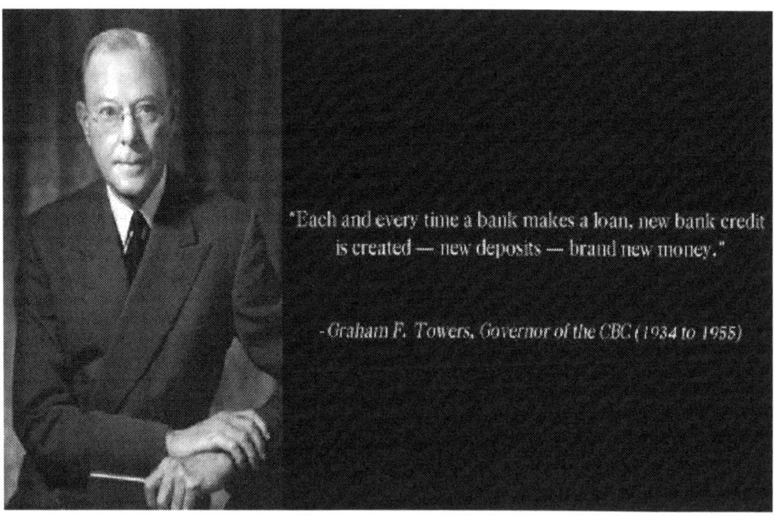

"Each and every time a bank makes a loan, new bank credit is created- new deposits - brand-new money."Graham F. Towers, Governor of the CBC Central Bank of Canada (1934 to 1955)

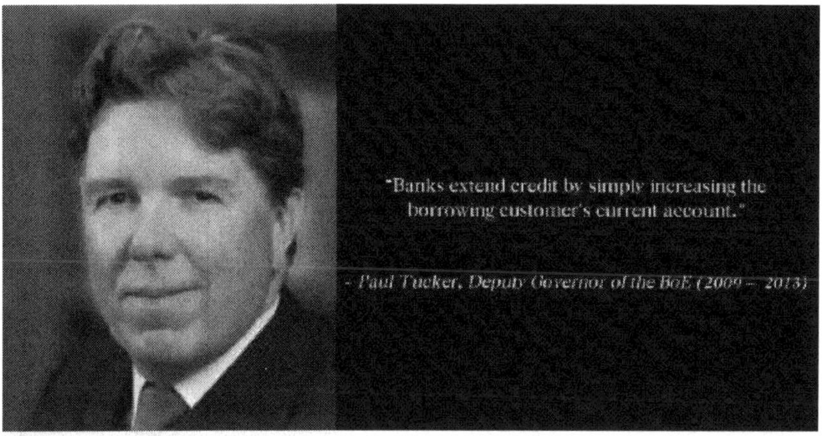

"Banks extend credit by simply increasing the borrowing customer's current account."-Paul Tucker, Deputy Governor of the Bank of England (BoE 2009 - 2013)

So, each time the bank makes a loan, it does not use the deposited money of other customers, it creates new money, in this day and time, it means typing new digits into a computer. 97% of all money is digitally created like this. Only 3% is the physical cash and coins that we carry.

(97% of all money is digital, only 3% is in the form of cash or coin currency) Banks can also lend out ten times more money than they actually have in reserves. This is called Fractional Reserve lending. This was the Federal Reserve Act System passed into law in 1913.

(U.S. Federal Reserve)

This is the same system used throughout the world. Printing more and more money causes inflation. In a way, inflation is an unfair tax that we all have to pay for the fraudulent creation of money. It is easy money printed now in exchange for the tax that must be paid for by our future generations. As long as this system is in place, things will always keep getting more expensive. In other words, this financial system is a "buy and enjoy everything today at the expense of tomorrow," system. This system creates debt money, but the money to pay the debt has not been created yet. At some point, the system will burst like an over inflated balloon.

> "If there were no debts in our money system, there wouldn't be any money."-Martinez Eccles, Governor of the Federal Reserve (Quoted 1941)

The system in which we live is a debt based monetary system in which debt always grows. In other words, countries and people must get deeper in debt so that there's more money in the system because debt is money and money is debt. If people and governments stop borrowing money and pay their debts, then the debt does not grow, the money supply shrinks and the system falters. We live and operate in this strange system every day.

The Federal Reserve and other central banks control money by adjusting its supply and dictating how much it costs to borrow money by controlling the interest rate. With these tools coupled with the consequence of human group psychology, central banks create "booms" and "busts" in the economy at will and can distort or derail an economy by tampering with it.

Here's a quick case study. In the year 2000 Federal Reserve Chairman, Alan Greenspan cut interest rates to 1%. This was allegedly done to prevent a recession from the "dot com" bubble (the downturn in the economy when the tech industry took a nosedive) and encouraged people to borrow more. When interest rates are low, if you are borrowing money, you save a lot when repaying mortgages. Since a 1% interest rate had not been seen since the 1950s, it was a great deal for people (or so they thought). The idea was that people would buy more houses, the value of their houses would then go up later on when the Fed raised interest rates again and people would feel richer and spend more money in the economy and stimulate it. Greenspan succeeded in getting people to borrow money to buy houses, but they borrowed too much and the result was the 2008 housing bubble.

(During the 2008 housing bubble, the housing market crashed, creating a recession)

This is a prime example of what can go wrong when the central banks mess with an economy. Corrupt banks played a huge role in the housing bubble recession and have a lot to answer for, but the privately owned Federal Reserve was at the center of the complete disaster! Without their bringing down of the interest rate to 1% and opening the floodgates on borrowing, the bubble never would have happened.

If the Fed never had lowered interest rates to 1% in 2001, the housing market collapse would not have taken place in 2008!

So in retrospect, it is the central bank which controls the economy, and it is the central bank combined with the commercial bank together which controls all of our money. The difference is, central banks can create money at will, while commercial banks need loans taken by their customers to create money.

"Permit me to issue and control the money of a nation, and I care not who makes its laws." -Mayer Amshcel Rothschild (Founder of the Rothschild family, international banking dynasty)

("Whoever controls the volume of money in any country is absolute master of all industry and commerce...when you realize that the entire system is very easily controlled, one way or another, by a few powerful men at the top, you will not have to be told how periods of inflation and depression originate." James A. Garfield, 20th President (Assassinated 1881)

In Benjamin Franklin's autobiography, he stated:

"The prime reason for the American war for independence was a battle over who actually controlled and issued the money to the new colonies."

Moving on to more recent times, Nobel Prize winning economist Milton Friedman states:

"The Federal Reserve definitely caused the Great Depression, by contracting the amount of currency in circulation by 1/3rd from 1929 to 1933."

The solution is that the government should fully own and control the money supply, not private bankers.

"The government should create, issue, and circulate all the currency and credits needed to satisfy the spending power of the Government and the buying power of consumers. By the adoption of these principles, the taxpayers will be saved immense sums of interest. Money will cease to be master and become the servant of humanity." - The 16th US President of the United States (February 12, 1809 – April 15, 1865) Abraham Lincoln was assassinated April 14, 1865

Abraham Lincoln had begun creating government owned currency, the greenback, 100% interest free.

(Debt free "Greenback money" printed by government to serve the people, not for the people to serve money)

All revolutions and all wars have their root causes in money. Smart people are starting to buy gold and other commodities instead of storing US dollars, anticipating the coming booms and busts of the global economy created by the privately owned Federal Reserve banksters (banking gangsters) and their cronies.

Chapter Three

False Education

Rather than guide students into the light of truth, the European/American education system (which Africa copies) is leading millions of young people into financial darkness and the worst type of slavery, servitude and debt. This is not by accident, but by design. The school teachers and university professors are also being duped by the same system. A curriculum which has been created by oppressors whose true aim is not to teach wealth creation but to produce generation after generation of graduates who are only fit for employment and are up to their necks in debt. Student loan debt. In America, student loan debt is over $1.2 trillion and is the most highly prized asset of the US Government. In the criminal world, this is called extortion, and I'll tell you why.

In the financial world, there are only two kinds of institutions which offer six-figure loans to 18-year-old students. 1) loan sharks and 2) colleges and universities. Please do not get me wrong. I do not oppose education. I have already said this in the introduction. But what I oppose is the total lack of financial intelligence education and a financial system designed to leave a student buried in debt with a degree which cannot even guarantee him a job after graduation. University education prepares students for employment. To be employees, not employers. This has been done deliberately. It is not wise to seek knowledge of how to obtain wealth from someone who is not wealthy and does not have aspirations of wealth creation. It is foolish to learn how to become self-employed from someone who is employed. Why should we learn economics from someone who is not a millionaire or in the very least financially stable? The following is an excerpt from the book "The Creature From Jekyll Island," by G Edward Griffin on Rockefeller's General Education Board, founded in 1903. (A book I suggest you read)

"The purpose of the foundation (the general education board) was to use the power of money, not to raise the level of education in America, as was widely believed at the time, but to influence the direction of that education... The object was to use the classroom to teach attitudes that encourage people to be passive and submissive to their rulers. The goal was-and is- to create citizens who were educated enough for productive work under supervision, but not enough to question authority or seek to rise above their class. True education was to be restricted to the sons and daughters of the elite. For the rest, it would be better to produce skilled workers with no particular aspirations other than to enjoy life."

It is obvious that there was and still is an ongoing plan to continue building institutions of learning, including universities, whose curriculums are designed to produce highly skilled slaves. Not purpose-driven people fulfilling their God-given destiny. Does this mean we should stop going to schools? The answer is no. What we should become however is wiser than our oppressors. Our teachers/professors are also stuck in the same system with jobs offering financial security (employment/slavery) not financial freedom. Most employees are stuck doing jobs they never liked or enjoy doing and most graduates are also stuck doing jobs totally unrelated to what they studied in the university and are still up to their necks in debt to the same universities which are in no position to guarantee jobs after graduation.

Here is some information you may find interesting about colleges and universities in America, as well as most of the civilized world. The vast majority of private and public universities and colleges are tax-exempt entities as defined by IRC section 501(C)(3) because of their educational purpose. Purposes that the government has long considered to be fundamental to fostering the productive and civic capacity of its citizens. Some of these institutions may be state or government entities. But football/sports tickets, textbook sales, food &

beverage sales, clothing sales, school accommodation, tuition etc. do not get taxed. This is a license to print money.

(Now 501(C)(3) is income from activities that are mostly related to the purpose of an institution's tax exemption, charitable contributions received, and investment income are not subject to federal income tax.)

Private and public schools do not pay taxes on:

- Property
- Tuition
- Sponsorships
- Donations
- Capital Gains (which are profits from sales).

One university, Rutgers University in New Brunswick, New Jersey, USA a public research university gets 26% in tuition and fees and an additional 22% in state appropriations from New Jersey state taxpayers. The 26% is $26,000 dollars multiplied by 70,000 Rutgers University students, which comes to $1.8 billion dollars on the lower side. This is Fortune 500 money. There are almost 2,000 publicly traded companies in the world with sales of $1 billion dollars or more. The 22% of state appropriations are actually state subsidies. This is taxpayer money coming out of the American taxpayers pocket in that state!

Rutgers University makes as much money as Tesla, the car manufacturing company with Elon Musk at its helm. Then the universities hoard the money. Then the universities organize non-stop donation drives and build huge hedge funds called endowments. Harvard University has an endowment fund of over $36 billion dollars, putting Harvard University on par with such nations as Bolivia as the 96th largest economy in the world. Based on information from the United Nations, there are over 100 countries with similar economies. With the money already in Harvard University's endowment fund, it could pay for 6,000 Harvard students tuition fees for 120 years for free. Meanwhile, student debt has increased and nearly doubled over the past ten years to $1.3 trillion U.S. dollars and rising.

Clearly there is a game being played in our educational system and those who do not understand the game will be played. Anyone who does not understand the rules of a game is bound to lose that game. That is the vast majority of all graduates coming out of universities, taking pictures with their families and celebrating the achievement of graduation only to enter into a system of capitalism with next to no financial intelligence education or even a basic understanding of the rules of the game of capitalism. This is a recipe for financial disaster for the graduates but maximum profits for the financial elite who want the status quo to continue for obvious reasons. In Kenya, Kenyatta University continues to build more and more modern buildings with funds coming from student's parents, most of whom are either farmers or struggling in the job sector. University school fees range from Kshs 100,000/- (roughly $1,000 USD) to Kshs 450,000/- (about $4,500 USD) depending on which course a student takes. This is a far cry from what students in the U.S. pay. The difference in the quality of education is also vast. But the result is often the same, a highly skilled, employable, passive, working class with no aspirations to move up in financial class, and no desire to question authority or the status quo.

In a story written in the Standard Online Newspaper by Fredrick Oginga, dated Thursday, March 14, 2019, titled "Young Educated but Jobless Years Later:" he writes: "Alfred Kibet Kirui, graduated with second class honors (lower division) degree in soil, water and environmental engineering from Jomo Kenyatta University of Agriculture and Technology last year. A week ago, Alfred became a topic of discussion when he hinted at killing himself over unemployment. He expressed frustration in his search for a job, narrating how his peers were ridiculing him. Ruth Rono, 27, from Baringo County also became the talk in most corners of the country after failing to get a job despite graduating with a First Class Honors degree from Chuka University three years ago.

Her sad story touched hearts, helping her land employment in one of the government corporations. It is Kibet's argument that a degree certificate is just a piece of paper, however, that has elicited sharp reactions from the public and brought to the fore a discussion on the state of our education system and its contribution to the soaring unemployment rate. Figures from institutions of higher learning show that slightly above 600,000 people are graduates, out of about 30 million Kenyans in the working-age bracket of between 15 and 64 years.

According to a survey done by the Kenya National Bureau of Statistics last year, seven million people - translating to about 7.4 percent of Kenyans - are unemployed, far from a 40 percent figure that has formed the talk in most conversations targeting the employment sector. Whereas the survey dismisses the argument that graduates from a huge population of the unemployed, it also paints another picture. That they are more when considering the number of young people actively searching for employment opportunities. It revealed that nine in every ten unemployed Kenyans are 35 years of age and below.

That is what seems to have befallen Martin Mutitu, who graduated from Kenyatta University in 2016 with a Bachelor of Education (Arts) degree. He says potential employers did not offer him more than Kshs 10,000 ($100 USD) a month salary. He decided to go back to college. "A graduate earning Kshs 10,000? How will I pay my bills? How will I eat? How will I send some money home?" He wonders. But even after graduating with a master's degree from the same institution, the situation has not changed. Mr. Mutitu, who still does menial jobs to survive, was last week on Friday pictured holding a placard along Nairobi's Thika Road near Ngara stage appealing to potential employers to give him a job. Opportunities for employment are at an all-time low, yet education institutions continue to graduate at least 50,000 graduates every year. This year, the country will have slightly above 90,000 students joining various colleges and universities. This means that even though the rate of employment is stagnating (meaning unemployment is rising), the number of graduates from our universities will double in five years to come.

Few Employers

The low number of companies and a difficult operating environment has also been mentioned as a factor contributing to graduate unemployment in the country. Parents sold all their land to educate them. Then you find them nagging their parents to still lend them money to prepare a CV for a job or kick-start a small business.

Almost every year, students in one Kenyan university or another pour out into the streets and riot over injustices for one reason or another. I believe that deep down inside they can tell they are being taken advantage of, but have no way of proving it or explaining it. They express their frustration by throwing stones and destroying property and this may not be the right way to have their voices heard, but society must accept that where there is smoke there is fire. The smoke of stone throwing and rioting is only an expression of the frustration felt by a student whose parents have sold everything they own and given their lives savings in order to send them to school, only to have their investment wasted in the fire of the miseducation and exploitation of the youth by the elite who know full well what they are doing and have absolutely no intention of changing anything, especially if it means the loss of power from their side. Lack of jobs leads to insecurity, insecurity leads to a reduction of foreign and local investment which further exacerbates the situation into a vicious cycle of poverty and exploitation. Straight from the devil's kitchen, comes the devil's soup.

The good news is that there are homeschool curriculums online for children and further education options for adults who may not be able to afford school fees. One can acquire a complete degree level education in 18 months with a laptop and a Wi-Fi connection. Everything in the world has moved on because of technology, except college and university education. How is that even possible? The truth is you have to go to school to be a doctor, lawyer or an engineer, a specialist, etc., but you do not have to go to college/university to be rich.

Teachers are teaching knowledge which is designed to make you a skilled employee. This curriculum is more like the devil's life-plan for students, e.g., get a job, buy a house, save money, and invest in a balanced portfolio of stocks, bonds and mutual funds. All of which is fake financial information. America and the world are harassed with strategically placed agents of false financial information designed to mislead the masses.

After graduation there are entire industries of gurus, advisors, and brokers who reinforce this fake financial advice while enriching themselves meanwhile. College and university education may be expensive, but self-education is priceless.

Real teachers do what they teach. A false teacher will teach on something they are not profiting from themselves. Almost like an obese fitness trainer. Your business professor in university is not a businessman. Why is that? The answer is simple. Your business professor teaches theory, not reality. Many graduates find themselves using very little of what they learned in the University in the real world of business.

This is because in today's world, knowledge advances every eighteen months. In other words, what you learned eighteen months ago may be obsolete tomorrow. Satan knows this and has cleverly designed an educational system which appears to produce results on the one hand but actually does more damage on the other. Sixty percent of university graduates in Kenya on average are still unemployed years after graduation. Fake education or useless information is what I call false light. 2 Corinthians 4:4 says,

> "In whom the god of this world has blinded the minds of them which believe not, lest the light of the glorious gospel of Christ, who is the image of God, should shine unto them."

Satan blinds the minds of the students with useless information. Before Satan was kicked out of Heaven, his name was "Lucifer." This name means "light bearer." He was a carrier of truth. But he sinned against God,

He attempted to overthrow the government of Heaven and was cast out by angels loyal to God. One cannot deceive if he does not know the truth. One who is ignorant of truth can only mislead, but he cannot deceive. To deceive, is to deliberately mislead with the intention of betrayal or destruction. Jesus said it in John 8:44

"...when he speaks a lie, he speaks of his own, for he is a liar, and the father of it."

Wherever we find deception being promoted, we know its originator is Satan, the god of this world. But he has already been judged, he is a defeated enemy that has no more power, except over those who are ignorant of God's word. Unfortunately, the vast majority of the world are ignorant of God's word. Satan thrives where there is no light. His number one goal around ignorance is to keep you ignorant of your identity. I am not attacking universities, I am simply opening the eyes of many who have put their trust in institutions of higher learning, not knowing what awaits them on the other side. Jesus shows you who you really are. True financial wealth is obtained when one discovers their purpose in life and begins fulfilling it.

In the following chapters, I will begin explaining step by step how one may obtain wealth. It is not a get-rich- quick scheme. It is not a "Ponzi scheme" or a pyramid scheme for that matter. Furthermore, it is simple biblical financial wisdom which can benefit anyone who applies these simple principles. They do require that one takes personal responsibility for their lives. Anyone who blames others for their position in life is only robbing themselves of the opportunity of taking personal responsibility for themselves, their financial future and having the self-determination to make a better future for themselves despite life's difficulties. By teaching people to become business owners and investors, they will discover a whole new world of financial abundance and opportunity. Without a solid financial education, one is forced to be a prisoner of employment. The following is a list of things people do not learn in school but are absolutely critical for financial success in life:

1. How to think
2. How to sell
3. How to negotiate
4. How to face failure
5. How to manage time
6. How to invest money
7. Principles of success
8. How to build a career
9. How to handle money
10. How to make an impact,
11. How to start a business
12. The importance of travel
13. How to be a good partner

14. How to read a financial statement
15. the laws and principles of capitalism,
16. the laws and principles of poverty
17. the laws and principles of wealth, its creation and its expansion and its preservation.

This list is not all that is required for financial freedom, but is definitely a start in the right direction. The journey of a thousand miles begins with a step. Jesus has taken many on this journey before you. You are no exception. Deuteronomy 8:18 says,

> "But thou shalt remember the Lord thy God: for it is He that gives you the power to get wealth, that He may establish His covenant which swore unto your fathers as it is this day."

Without the knowledge of these fundamental areas of financial intelligence we can expect more unemployment, more frustration, increased crime, a rise in HIV/AIDS as immorality increases and many other social calamities.

It has become abundantly clear to me that the first nation that adopts a comprehensive financial education program for all students, rich or poor, will emerge as a financial world power. I predict that the country that provides the best bible based financial education for their students will lead the world into a new era of economic prosperity.

Chapter Four

Rules of The Game

In a world where most people worship money, financial wisdom is absolutely critical. The scriptures teach about money and how it may be acquired without compromising one's integrity. Proverbs 24: 3-6 says,

> "Through wisdom is a house built and by understanding it is established: And by knowledge, shall the chambers be filled with all precious and pleasant riches. A wise man is strong: yea, a man of knowledge increases strength. For by wise counsel thou shalt make thy war: and in multitude of counselors there is safety."

College and University graduates are attempting to declare war on poverty but are ill-equipped to do so with their university degrees and certifications which do not result in financial freedom but instead can only offer financial security (employment) which is slavery at the end of the day. Too many people have thought about starting their own business, but because of fear of the unknown have refused to step out of the boat and walk on the financial waters. Many people lack faith.

"So then faith comes by hearing, and hearing by the word of God." (Romans 10:17)

Unfortunately, the truth is that people are afraid to try because deep down inside they fear losing more than they desire winning. People who avoid the risk of investment would rather have a steady paycheck (financial security) than great wealth and their own business (financial freedom). What they fail to understand is that money is similar to a game, the more you play, the better you get. But school has taught you not to make mistakes. By punishing you for making mistakes instead of teaching you to learn from your mistakes and get better, you are robbed of one of the major building blocks of wealth creation which is, learning through experience. Capitalism is a "horse and jockey" system. The horse does all the work and the jockey gets all the credit. The unfortunate truth about capitalism is that those who are financially disciplined and knowledgeable will benefit from those who are not. This is because investing is basically a transfer of wealth from those who are impatient to those who are patient. Patience is one of the fruits of the Spirit, found in Galatians 5:22"but the fruit of the Spirit is love, joy, peace, long-suffering (patience), gentleness, goodness, faith, meekness (self-control), temperance against such there is no law."

Financial patience is one of the fruits which can produce wealth, since investment is a transfer of wealth from those who are in a financial hurry to those who are not. People who have not been trained on how to deal with money usually do not know how to earn it, how to keep it or how to grow it. Governments are more keen to take care of those who

1. Own property instead of renting.
2. Run companies instead of working for other people.
3. Produce rather than consume.
4. Lend instead of borrowing or borrow to develop property.
5. Invest rather than spend.

As of 2018, Kenya's Gross Domestic Product (GDP) is about $85.98 billion USD. GDP is simply the volume of economic activity within a country. The per capita GDP is calculated by taking the total GDP and dividing it by the country's population. This means that Kenya's per capita GDP in 2018 averaged somewhat more than $1,790 USD annually. That is the average amount of money which every Kenyan earned in the year 2018 if every Kenyan made the same amount. That is roughly $149.2 USD per month. About Kshs 15,000 per month is what the average Kenyan is earning. It is my belief that as a people, we can do a lot better. If this nation (Kenya) has even produced a United States president, (Barack Obama) there is no telling what else we can do.

> "Our goal for the black race is to make them into a reliable, hardworking, well-disciplined, noncompetitive subordinated labor force." - Unknown Source

In order for one to have financial wisdom, one must first understand the law of knowledge. The law of knowledge states that;

> "If I know more than you, then you must pay me, BUT if you know more than me, then I must pay you. Period."

After a statement like that, everyone should be packed inside libraries across the country. Instead, many spend hours seated in front of the television staring at a box being amused instead of sharpening their minds and researching to find out what kind of problem they can solve in society. The billionaires of tomorrow are the problem solvers of today. What problem do you intend to use your gifts and talents to solve? What solution will you offer humanity in exchange for their money? If you want to make money, understand that you will have to get it from people.

Money is usually given in exchange for goods and services. Money has quite a few definitions depending on how you view it. According to Google's dictionary, money is defined as: "a current medium of exchange in the form of coins and banknotes." That is a layman's definition of money. From an investor's perspective, money is a pathway for the development of capital and infrastructure. In an efficient market, money should be placed in its most productive position. In other words, poor people earn money. Rich people control money. There is a powerful difference between the way these two people view money. Rich people know the difference between Cash Flow and Capital Gains.

Cash Flow is better than Capital Gains. If you buy a house and sell it for a profit, the profit is called Capital Gains. The government taxes Capital Gains less than employees' salaries and yet, those who make money from Capital Gains earn far more!

Cash Flow is however better because Cash Flow from the same house can be obtained by putting tenants into that house and collecting rents every month. Cash Flow keeps putting money into your pocket. But in order to invest for Cash Flow, one must first acquire capital. In America, it is easier to obtain capital than it is in Africa, but that does not mean it is impossible. In America if one has a good credit score (a good reputation of borrowing and paying debts on time, e.g. a documented history of financial discipline) one can get a loan and start a business investing in real estate for cash flow (an example of good debt). In Africa, the credit bureau system is yet to come to the forefront of economic activity, but it is quickly getting there and will be a factor of African economics in the foreseeable future. Again this deals with the principle of faithfulness.

> *"Moreover, it is required in stewards, that a man be found faithful."* (1Corinthians 4:2)

If you can be trusted, you can become rich. Investors all over the world are looking for people who can be trusted. The U.S. housing crisis of 2007/2008 was caused by people who could not be trusted with one of America's most powerful sources of wealth. Their homes. The result was the collapse of the U.S. housing market. Bear Stearns, the global investment bank, collapsed and was sold to JPMorgan Chase for $10 dollars per share. Lehman Brothers, the financial services firm, filed for bankruptcy, becoming the largest bankruptcy filing case in U.S. history.

Lehman was holding over $600 billion USD in assets. The subprime mortgage crisis left it especially vulnerable to any reduction in real estate values. The major cause of the financial collapse of the U.S. housing markets was greed. People on Wall Street like to use big words to confuse laymen, but the simple explanation of why the housing market collapsed is because people (big financial institutions) were betting that people who had no ability to pay their debts would actually pay. A bank would take its subprime mortgages (home loans offered to high-risk borrowers with low credit scores and thus higher interest rates) and sell them to another financial institution (as a financial tool) which would then package them with other subprime mortgages from other financial institutions and hedge (insure/protect) them using insurance companies like American International Group (AIG). The insurance company pays the debt if the debtor defaults and/or is unable to pay. AIG was the world's biggest insurer, but was bailed out by the U.S. government to the tune of $85 billion dollars of taxpayer money. If AIG had not been bailed out, it would have gone bankrupt. Its bankruptcy would have damaged the U.S. economy. The U.S. government decided that AIG was "too big to fail." In exchange, the U.S. government received nearly 80% of AIG's equity.

A financial vehicle which is derived from another financial vehicle is called a derivative. These subprime mortgage financial products were called derivatives. An example of a derivative can be orange juice. Orange juice is a derivative of oranges. Grape juice and wine are derivatives of grapes. Credit default swaps were simply derivatives of subprime mortgage products which were simply bad debts which could not be paid by borrowers. The people who accepted the debt (homes) could not be trusted to pay for the homes, and a quick look at their credit scores would have confirmed this. As a result, one thing led to another and the entire market collapsed.

There were those who knew that the market would collapse and bet against the market. Leading many to believe that this entire Ponzi scheme was engineered from the very top. The elite CEOs of the biggest financial institutions involved in the housing bubble Ponzi scheme were bailed out with taxpayer money and the CEOs awarded themselves with higher salaries, more cash bonuses worth millions of dollars and more equity also worth millions in the very companies they almost brought down. In the end, one thing is certain and all of that has been said to prove this one point - *the tax-payer loses*. Wall Street was bailed out by Main Street. The hardest working people in America and around the world were robbed by those who work the least. Very many people committed suicide as a result of the collapse of the housing market, as people lost their homes in droves. Suddenly, fortunes were lost, entire life savings vanished into thin air. Tens of thousands of people were left financially ruined. The ripple effect of the downturn was felt all over the world.

In a story written by Melanie Haiken in Forbes dated June 12, 2014, more than 10,000 suicides were linked to the economic crisis. She wrote: "A dramatic spike in suicides between 2008 and 2010 can be linked with the economic crisis, according to a study published today in the British Journal of Psychiatry. Researchers from the University of Oxford compared suicide data from before 2007 with the years of the crisis and found more than 10,000 "economic suicides" associated with the recession across the U.S., Canada and Europe." Thousands of people who had put their trust in money and financial systems were suddenly let down. They could not handle the loss of their homes or their money, and the ripple effect it had in their lives was too much for them to handle. The actual number of economic downturn related deaths is not known, but it is definitely into the hundreds of thousands. The hardest-hit community by the 2008 housing market crash was the black American community. The enemy knew this and sent millions of spirits of depression to those who were hit the hardest by the housing market collapse. The result was thousands of untimely deaths. Very few people actually understand what even took place during the housing market crisis. The language was designed to keep ordinary people out. One of the objectives of the financial industry is to keep ordinary people confused.

Oftentimes wherever there is confusion there is deception, but wherever there is simplicity there is truth. A wise man once said, "simplicity is genius."

Anywhere you see theft, destruction and death, you know that Satan's fingerprints were all over the crime scene. Satan engineered the entire housing crisis. He intends to engineer more financial crises in the future. He knows that finances are directly tied to a person's wellbeing. Without money, one is exposed to all kinds of evil.

> "For wisdom is a defense and money is a defense: but the excellency of knowledge is, that wisdom gives life to them that have it." (Ecclesiastes 7:12)

Those who put their trust in money are not wise. Financial ignorance is a vital component of the conspiracy of the rich. Going to school, getting a job, buying a home, saving money, staying free of debt and investing in a diversified portfolio of stocks, bonds and mutual funds is NOT a good financial plan. The reason this plan is so dangerous is that it sounds good but is actually toxic. Satan's lies are dangerous because they sound like the truth, but he slips in a little lie to get you hooked and then by the time you find out, you've already been duped.

I cannot overemphasize how important it is for anyone seeking financial wisdom to understand why you must legally avoid paying too much in taxes at all costs. Unfortunately, employees are hit by the government the hardest and pay the most in taxes percentage wise. Over and over again, we see that taxpayers are left holding the bill whenever financial big shots feel like lining their pockets with taxpayer money. In Kenya, employees earning over Kshs 47,059 per month are taxed at 30%. This means that during an entire working year, 3.6 months will be spent working completely for the government for free. The rest of the money earned in salaries will be distributed to various service providers, e.g. your landlord, your water, your electricity, your food, your cell phone (airtime) your transportation, your children's school fees, your entertainment, your grooming (haircuts, hair & nail salon etc.) and other liabilities leaving you almost broke by the end of the month. Only for the new month to arrive, and the entire process starts all over again. Those with financial wisdom understand that we live in an unjust financial system designed to enrich the few at the expense of the many. Although there may be little we can do to change the system, there is a lot you can do to change yourself.

In yet another financial taxpayer money related scandal, members of the National Social Security Fund could lose Kshs 11.5 Billion in the Hazina Tower project.

(Photo taken by Nation Media Group, used for educational purposes)

This image taken on March 12, 2014, shows the stalled construction of Hazina Trade Centre in Nairobi.

In a story published by the daily nation newspaper online edition dated Friday, March 23, 2018, journalist Samuel Owino writes:

> "Taxpayers are losing a whopping Kshs 20,000,000 per week ... now about 2.5million members who contribute to the fund could be left Kshs 11.5 Billion short with only a stump of the skyscraper to show for it in what has the makings of an unraveling scandal.

MPs have now ordered that only minimal work should continue at the construction site in a bid to save taxpayers the loss of billions of shillings as controversy continues to dog the building that could have been one of the iconic structures in the city."

Needless to say, the taxpayer loses again. This is not just a unique situation in Kenya. The biggest taxpayers all over the world are usually the biggest financial losers. These "losers" are called employees.

Don't get me wrong, employees are great, hard-working people. My own father was an employee most of his working life. But when he found his identity in Christ, he was able to evolve from being an employee in the United States to being a pastor of one of the largest churches in the Kiambu district, Father's House Family Church. He is more fulfilled and loves what he does. My mother and father showed me that once you meet Jesus, (through learning the word of God) you begin to realize who you are and when your true identity is revealed to you, you break out of the chains of slavery and cross over to the winning side of wisdom for life, and you begin to see what you could not see before. This is what it means to "see the light." Light is knowledge. I'm not telling you to quit your job and start a church, I'm telling you to find your purpose and do it.

"And ye shall know the truth, and the truth shall make you free." (John 8:32)

Please do not get me wrong, I am not telling you to quit your job and stop paying taxes. I am encouraging you to learn the system in which you live and realize who you are in Christ, and then begin to take the steps of transforming mentally from a slave to a son of a King.

". . . and be not conformed to this world, but be ye transformed by the renewing of your mind, that ye may prove, what is that good and acceptable and perfect will of God." (Romans 12:2)

Is it the will of God that you should be wasting your life away contributing to a system that keeps showing you that it is designed to fail? A December 11, 2018, Nation Online News story revealed that detectives had unearthed a Kshs 50 Billion scam at the National Hospital Insurance Fund (NHIF). NHIF management and some hospital administrators conspired to double-charge the government in medical bills. This scheme left patients dying as unscrupulous administrators and government treasury officials made off with billions in taxpayer money.

Is this not modern-day slavery? Read Jesus' words again.

"Come unto me, all ye that labor and are heavy laden, and I will give you rest. Take my yoke upon

> *you, and learn of me, for I am meek and lowly in heart: and ye shall find rest unto your souls. For my yoke is easy, and my burden is light." Matthew 11:28)*

Pay extra attention to the words "take my yoke upon you and learn of me". This financial system has been designed to keep men enslaved. The system is doing what it is designed to do - it enriches the few at the expense of the many. Do not be surprised that it does this. This is exactly how Pharaoh enslaved the children of Israel for 400 years in Egypt. Without financial wisdom, the system will enslave you, but with wisdom you can come out from the masses and become great. Proverbs 8:11-18 says,

> "For wisdom is better than rubies; and all things that may be desired are not to be compared to it. I, Wisdom, dwell with prudence and find out knowledge of witty inventions. The fear of the Lord is to hate evil, pride and arrogance, and the evil way, and the froward mouth do I hate.

Counsel is mine, and sound wisdom: I am understanding, I have strength. By me kings reign and princes decree justice. By me princes rule, and nobles, even all the judges of the earth. I love them that love me and those that seek me early will find me. Riches and honor are with me, yea durable riches and righteousness."

Most pastors find it difficult to explain what I have just explained to you about your purpose relating to the financial system in which we live. The word of God assures us that it is possible to have durable riches and righteousness. That is a beautiful combination because it assures your eternal life after you leave this earth in righteousness and improves your life while you are here with riches, so you can make huge Heavenly investments easing the suffering of others while living an abundant life while still here on earth. Wisdom guarantees this. Verses 20 and 21 of the same chapter says,

> *"I lead in the way of righteousness, in the midst of the paths of judgement. That I may cause those that love me to inherit substance; and I will fill their treasures."*

I don't have to promote the prosperity gospel message. I prefer the wisdom and righteousness message because it brings better results.

Prosperity without righteousness is dangerous. An American rapper named Mac Miller real name Malcolm McCormick had a net worth of $9,000,000USD but was found unresponsive in his Studio City home by his personal assistant who called

911 and performed CPR until paramedics arrived. It is believed that he died of an accidental drug overdose. This was a young and very "prosperous" man, but drugs destroyed his life. The availability of resources made drugs easily available, and it was this addiction to drugs that killed him. Although his untimely death was tragic, there is much we can learn from him. Riches without self-control and character can kill. There are many drug addicts who are broke, and it is good that they are broke because if they had an endless supply of money and drugs, they would be dead. For some people, poverty is actually a good thing. Alcoholism is also a destroyer of destiny and purpose. Those who are enslaved by its bondage need deliverance, or they will never achieve God's plan and purpose for their lives. This is the worst thing that can ever happen to someone. Financial wisdom demands that one uses wisdom in the way they handle money.

> *"Honor the Lord with your substance and with the first fruit of all your increase. So shall your barns be filled with plenty, and your presses burst out with new wine." (Proverbs 3:9)*

This verse has more than one meaning. Honoring the Lord with your substance means giving to God's work, giving to the poor and educating the hopeless, but it also means honoring God with how you spend your money. What you invest in shows who you are and what you truly believe in.

> *"For where your treasure is, there will your heart be also." (Matthew 6:22)*

Jesus is simply saying that people invest in what they believe in. Then they begin to receive a return on their investment. The return on the investment towards sin is death. The return on the investment towards time spent studying is a bright mind, sharper than the minds which have not invested time studying. One of the principles of increase is investment and return on investment. Money, in the hands of a righteous manager, will multiply. In other words, money multiplication is the right thing to do with money, this is the essence of asset management.

Wisdom in the area of finances begins with the smallest change in the way one views themselves and their resources. The following chapters are a simple step-by-step guide to help you raise the capital you need to begin your journey towards financial freedom.

> *"A good man leaves an inheritance to his children's children: and the wealth of the sinner is laid up for the just." (Proverbs 13:22)*

If you can barely pay your own bills, how will you leave an inheritance for your children and your children's children? The path towards wealth is a path of personal transformation.

It is gradual and not instantaneous, but the rewards are worth the time and effort put into it. You may be working at a job which has nothing to do with your purpose in life, but don't quit immediately (unless the job involves sin, then I would advise that you stop immediately). Continue working, but begin planning your escape.

Escape from prison is not a one-day operation. In the movie "Shawshank Redemption" the lead character Andy Dufresne (played by Tim Robbins), a banker, is sentenced to life imprisonment in Shawshank state penitentiary for the murder of his wife and her lover despite his claims of innocence. Over the next 20 years in prison he befriends a fellow prisoner, Ellis "Red" Redding (played by Morgan Freeman). Red is a contraband (illegal items) smuggler in the prison. Andy overheard the captain of the guards, Byron Hadley, complaining about being taxed on an inheritance and offered to help him shelter the money legally. Andy then begins handling financial matters for other prison staff, guards at other prisons, and the warden himself. He also begins writing weekly letters to the state legislature requesting funds to improve the prison's poorly equipped library. Andy explains to his friend Red that hope is what gets him through his time. Red does not believe in hope and dismisses his friend's sentiments. Then Norton, the head prison warden, begins exploiting prison labor for public works, profiting by undercutting skilled labor costs and receiving bribes. Andy launders (illegally "cleans" the money by making it appear as legitimate income) for the warden under the false name Randal Stephens.

Andy was innocent of the murders, but was punished for them nonetheless. Then one day during roll call, the guards find Andy's cell empty. Norton, the warden, gets so angry he throws a rock at a poster hanging on Andy's prison cell wall. The rock passes right through the poster into a hole in the prison wall which Andy had dug using his tiny rock hammer over the past 19 years. He used a rope which he had borrowed to escape through the tunnel and prison sewage pipe, taking the warden's suit, shoes and ledger, containing proof of the money laundering. Then Andy goes to the banks posing as Randal Stephens, withdraws the laundered money from several banks, and mails the ledger and other evidence of all the corruption and murders at Shawshank to a local newspaper. State police arrive at Shawshank and take prison authorities into custody. Norton, the prison warden commits suicide to avoid arrest.

After serving 40 years, Red is finally paroled. He finds life on the outside of prison to be difficult and fears he will never adjust. Then he remembers a promise he had made to Andy and visits Buxton and finds a cache containing money and a letter asking him to come and meet Andy in Mexico. As Red crosses the U.S./Mexico border, he finally admits that he feels some hope. He finds Andy on a beach and the two friends happily embrace.

One can draw much wisdom from this story. Life can sometimes sentence you and punish you for crimes you may have not committed. But how you respond to life's setbacks is what separates the winners from the losers. Red had given up hope and was willing to just accept whatever life offered to him. Andy on the other hand was different. Andy made a plan and began working on that plan over the next 19 years. His patience was tested, so was his drive and his determination. He kept hammering away bit by bit at the wall in his prison room until finally the hole was big enough to fit through. He then prepared for the future, calculated every step, knowing that what he was doing was right. Furthermore, he had been imprisoned for a crime he did not commit, the system which had imprisoned him did not care whether he was guilty or not. It was a ruthless beast designed to exploit the powerless, all the while posing as a just and honest system. Andy knew the system was his enemy, but it could also be used for his benefit depending on how he used it. Andy studied the system. He spent time in the library, reading and sharpening his mind. He understood the law of knowledge, for if I know more than you, then you must pay me, but if you know more than me, then I must pay you. Andy became the star of the library. By the time he escaped the prison, he knew more than the prison wardens. He knew more than his fellow inmates. He knew more than his old self. This was a new Andy; and this was Andy transformed!

> "And be not conformed to this world, but be thou transformed by the renewing of your mind: that ye may prove what is that good, and acceptable and perfect will of God." (Romans 12:2)

There is a hidden wisdom, which most people don't know of. A hidden wisdom is prepared for those who will search for it and desire it and pay the price of time spent studying and searching for it consistently until they find it. A more profound wisdom hidden from "on the surface Christians," who have no real relationship with their bible and never bother to dig deep. A wisdom, prepared for kings, not for those who find bible study boring. Dangerous wisdom described in 1 Corinthians 1:21-24 is this,

> *"For after that in the wisdom of God the world by wisdom (its own wisdom) knew not God, it pleased God by the foolishness of preaching to save them that believe. For the Jews require a sign and the Greeks seek after wisdom (the wisdom of the gods, fallen angels): But we speak Christ crucified, unto*

the Jews a stumbling block and unto the Greeks, foolishness; But unto them which are called, both Jews and Greeks, Christ the power of God, and the wisdom of God.

There is an astronomical amount of wisdom hidden in Christ, which the whole world's system despises. Just like warden Norton despising the hidden wisdom of Andy. But the hidden wisdom in Christ is something the world refuses to take into account and has not yet considered to even be a threat.

"It is the glory of God to conceal a thing: but the honor of kings is to search out a matter."(Proverbs 5:2)

"...that is, Christ Himself, in whom are hidden all the treasures of wisdom and knowledge." (Colossians 2:3,4)

If you are not searching, you will never become the king you were born to be. The world despises Christ and does not consider him to be a threat. That is bad news for them, but it is good news for us who are saved.

"Howbeit we speak wisdom among them that are perfect; yet not the wisdom of this world, nor of the princes of this world, that come to naught: But we speak the wisdom of God in a mystery, even the

hidden wisdom, which God ordained before the world unto our glory: Which none of the princes of this world knew: for had they known it, they would not have crucified the Lord of glory." (1 Corinthians 2:6-8)

Had the fallen angels known the hidden wisdom of God, they never would have crucified the Lord Jesus Christ. They never understood the principles of righteousness, judgement and equity described in Proverbs 2:9.

"Then shalt thou understand righteousness, and judgement and equity; yea, every good path."

But they unjustly accused and sentenced Jesus to death. They violated the principles of equity and righteousness. Judgement followed immediately afterwards. Jesus sued Satan in the eternal courts of justice for gross injustice, inequity and lack of judgement. The Father found Jesus not guilty of the crimes Satan accused him of. Crimes which, as far as Satan was concerned, were worthy of death. Jesus was so shrewd. He knew the principle of rulership.

"It is an abomination for kings to commit wickedness: for the throne is established by righteousness." (Proverbs 16:12)

Jesus sued for Satan's throne because Satan had used his position of power to commit injustice. Jesus, who was found not guilty by God, the Eternal Judge, of crimes punishable by death proceeded to sue Satan for all manner of punitive damages including, wrongful death, conspiracy to commit murder, conspiracy to defraud and obtain goods by false pretenses (they had taken his clothing and sold it), false accusation, etc. and the list goes on and on. Needless to say, Jesus won the case, his sacrificial death was allowed to be payment for the sins of the whole world and Jesus was given Satan's throne, the very throne which Adam had. Satan outsmarted Adam and took his throne, his crown and his title, but Jesus outsmarted Satan, and legally took back the throne and the crown and the title. Then God judged Satan and found him guilty on all counts. Satan was given what can be compared to a deferred sentence. A deferred sentence is a sentence that is suspended until after a defendant has completed a period of probation. If the defendant fulfills the stipulations surrounding probation, a judge may then throw out the sentence and guilty plea, clearing the incident from their record. But Satan is so evil and foolish. He continues to violate people and do all kinds of evil even during his probation period. This time we are in now is that probation period. Satan is the temporary banker of this world.

He prints the money and writes oppressive policies designed to oppress the children of God as much as possible while enriching his own children at our expense. Satan, (through his 13 bloodline banking family children) prints dollars through the privately owned Federal Reserve. He then manipulates the global markets to further oppress the masses while enriching his own wicked children. He is able to do this by increasing and decreasing the money supply and then positioning his children who know what is coming next in the market (because they make it happen) to trade against the coming trend, thereby profiting handsomely at the expense of everyone else. This can be explained easily by the following simple example.

Imagine everyone is on a ship. But there are only a few life jackets on this ship. Then a shrewd life jacket salesman is asked what to do. He quietly puts a hole in the bottom of the ship so that the ship begins sinking. Then he begins to announce that the ship is sinking, and life jackets are for sale to the highest bidder. The fearful cash rich passengers offer everything they have for the life jackets, the cash poor passengers are excluded from the game and heartbroken. The value of the jackets remains the same, but the price of the life jackets sky-rocket because of high demand combined with short supply. After the jackets are sold, the shrewd businessman goes back down and repairs the ship with tools and a repair team he had already prepared in advance. The ship is no longer sinking and the prices of the life jackets go back to normal, but the masses have already transferred their wealth and are left with overpriced life jackets and a bad taste in their mouths.

Then the life jacket salesman splits the profits with the repairmen, the captain of the ship and the life jacket distributors. This is the power of a wicked partnership. This is what Satan does in the marketplace every day. He excludes billions of poor people by not allowing them to participate in the global marketplace, he swindles unsuspecting students, he coerces leaders, enslaves taxpayers and manipulates governments and defrauds them of their money. All over the world, there are wicked partnerships who are patiently waiting while white-collar thugs in key banking positions steal hardworking people's money.

> *"A prudent man foresees the evil, and hides himself: but the simple pass on and are punished."(Proverbs 22:3)*

Chapter Five

A Crash Course in Capitalism

"Everything you want to know about the world, you can know by following the money." - Ronald Bernard (ex banker, asset management, deposit trading, Netherlands)

MONEY is defined as a current medium of exchange in the form of coins and banknotes; coins and banknotes collectively.

CAPITALISM is defined as: "an economic and political system in which a country's trade and industry are controlled by private owners for profit, rather than by the state."

If capitalism is controlled by private owners, then there are indeed a few who are enriched at the expense of the many. Capitalism as a term was popularized by Karl Marx in the 19th century. However, the principles of Capitalism were laid out by a Scottish philosopher named Adam Smith in 1776. In his treatise "An Enquiry Into the Nature and Causes of the Wealth of Nations." Smith advocated what we call the free market economy and put into writing what had been already happening for centuries elsewhere. In Abyssinia (modern-day Africa), Mansa Musa (or the tenth "Musa" or "Sultan," "Conqueror") was the leader of the wealthy west African Mali empire. Musa conquered 24 cities. During his reign, Mali may have been the largest producer of gold in the world. Musa was one of the wealthiest people in history. Time magazine reported: "there's really no way to put an accurate number on his wealth. Solomon, the son of David, was the wisest king that ever lived.

> "Now the weight of gold which came in to Solomon in one year was 666 talents of gold, besides that from the traders and the wares of the merchants and all the kings of the Arabs and the governors of the country." (1Kings 10:14)

A talent of gold was roughly the same as the weight of a person. Around 50 kgs. Today, one kilogram of gold is about $40,968.09 USD. That is about 33,300 kgs of gold which translates to about $1,364,237,397 USD (One billion, three hundred and sixty-four million, two hundred and thirty-seven thousand, three hundred and ninety-seven USD) per year in today's money. This kind of money coming in over 4,000 years ago was a colossal sum. And this was besides that which came in from the traders and wares of the merchants and all the kings of the Arabs and the governors of the country.

After the discovery of the "New World," (America), trade became big business. Capitalism has four basic principles.

They are:

1. Business Capital is privately owned
2. Buyers and Sellers control the economy
3. Business owners and workers have free will to spend their money on whatever they desire
4. Minimal government oversight

This was called "Laissez faire:" or "hands off" and "let be." But with no government regulation, employers took advantage of workers with long hours, dangerous working environments and abuse of child labor. Capitalism set the foundation for slavery, even though slavery predates the term "capitalism." Zero government regulation clearly allows oppression. Generally, capitalism is amazingly productive, but has two major flaws.

1. Firstly, it is systematically inclined to ignore the suffering of workers unless regularly supervised and prodded not to.
2. Secondly, the wealth of companies is built on satisfying what are not the essential needs of human beings. Fortunes are made through the sale of unhealthy food, evil television programs, bad news, etc.

The challenge for the future, therefore, is how we may be able to make money humanely, without oppressing anyone and still treating the people and the earth with care, as well as making money by addressing the noble and virtuous side of human needs. Jesus made a whip and drove out the money changers from the temple.

Not because he disagreed with business, but because they were turning matters of sin and forgiveness into big business. Matthew 21:12,13 says this:

> *"Then Jesus entered the temple and drove out all who were selling and buying in the temple, and he overturned the tables of the money changers and the seats of those who sold doves. He said to them, "It is written, 'My house shall be called a house of prayer'; but you are making it a den of robbers."*

The doves they sold in the temple were for the purposes of offering for certain sins, and the money was being changed from foreign currencies to local currency for the purpose of buying sin offerings. So, they had corrupted atonement and made forgiveness of sin a matter of buying and selling. Jesus hates that the money changers were making merchandise of travelers who had come from far, some with honest hearts, only to be taken advantage of by temple traders. The Catholic

Church made fortunes from selling the forgiveness of sins in the form of "indulgences" during the 16th century and is still corrupt to the core till this day. In many ways, the kingdom of darkness always tries to find a way to corrupt and exploit the children of God. Capitalism has owners who have conspired to exploit and corrupt the children of God all over the world.

Just like Andy (from the Shawshank Redemption movie discussed earlier) we must conspire against the powers that be which have been conspiring against us for hundreds of years. If you have not yet realized that there is a conspiracy to oppress the masses and keep them poor and desperate, then you need to open your eyes. The power of sin is in its secrecy. When you realize how you have been sinned against by the god of this world, his bloodlines and their children's children through ungodly capitalism, a certain righteous indignation should arise within you.

> *"Wherefore he saith, awake thou that sleeps, and arise from the dead, and Christ shall give you light." (Ephesians 5:14 KJV)*

That light which Christ gives is the knowledge of reality. The Spirit of truth, which is His spirit.

> *"Have nothing to do with the fruitless deeds of darkness, but rather expose them."Ephesians 5:11* - NIV

This is the reason my wife and I expose the synagogue of Satan and reveal what is happening to you so that you can have an upper hand and build a life worth living.

On the cover of this book is a picture of an image inscribed on the United States one-dollar bill. It is filled with meaning yet shrouded in secrecy. The eagle is the symbol of the various nations of Esau.

Obadiah 1:4 says,

> "The vision of Obadiah. Thus saith the Lord God concerning Edom; We have heard a rumors from the Lord, and an ambassador is sent among the heathen, arise ye, and let us rise up against her in battle. Behold, I have made thee small among the heathen: thou art greatly despised. The pride of thine heart has deceived you, thou that dwells in the clefts of the rock, whose habitation is high; that saith in his heart, who shall bring me down to the ground? Though thou exalt thyself as the EAGLE, and though thou set thy nest among the stars, thence will I bring thee down, saith the Lord."

This is God's message to Edom. We know that Edom is Esau from Genesis 36:1: *"Now these are the generations of Esau, who is Edom."*

So, the nations symbolized by the eagle are Edom which is Esau, the brother of Jacob. The nations of Edom include; The United States, Germany, Rome, Poland, Romania and Egypt etc. Today we are in the latter Roman Empire. Rome (the Vatican) wields considerable power over the world and presidents of nations all over the world including the U.S. presidents visit the Pope and acknowledge his status and power in today's world. This is not by coincidence. The Catholic Church proper is the great whore described in Revelation 17:1-2,

> *"And there came one of the seven angels which had the seven vials, and talked with me, saying unto me, come hither; I will show unto you the great judgement of the great whore that sits upon many waters: With whom the kings of the earth have committed fornication, and the inhabitants of the earth have been made drunk with the wine of her fornication."*

The word "Catholic" means universal, which means all-inclusive. In other words, the Catholic Church has included all forms of religion into its doctrines and mixed them with

Christianity. The bible calls this whoredom. But whoredom involves money, the sale of that which should never be sold, e.g. selling forgiveness of sin, favor with God, etc. All the various gods are included and accepted to be worshiped by the Vatican. The apostasy of the Catholic Church is what revelation 17 calls whoredom and fornication. This has everything to do with us today because this system of Rome, which is an extension of Ancient Egypt, is enslaving the whole world under its financial system. The nations of Edom benefit most from this system at the expense of Jacob.

Please remember that Jacob was blessed by Isaac in Genesis 27:27-29

> *"And he (Jacob) came near and kissed him: and he smelled the smell of his raiment, and blessed him, and said, See, the smell of my son is as the smell of a field which the Lord hath blessed: Therefore God give thee of the dew of heaven, and the fatness of the earth, and plenty of corn and wine: Let people serve thee, and nations bow down to thee: cursed be everyone that curses thee, and blessed be he that blesses thee."*

If one looks closely, the nations across Africa are always being oppressed and plundered to the benefit of the west. There is an ongoing steady stream of natural resources flowing from Africa at far below western market value into western markets including gold, coltan (used for production of tantalum capacitors, used in almost all the world's electronic devices, e.g. mobile phones etc.), silver, uranium, diamonds, oil and natural gas deposits, platinum, copper, iron, bauxite and more. Can you see the blessing which Isaac spoke over Jacob in the sheer wealth of our natural resources?

> *"Therefore God give thee of the dew of heaven, and the fatness of the earth, and plenty of corn and wine:" Genesis 27:28*

The fatness of the earth is the wealth that the earth can produce. But the people who live in these resource rich African countries are excluded from enjoying the wealth produced in their lands. This is classic slavery and oppression, the same oppression we saw in Egypt when the children of Israel were enslaved by Pharaoh. Pharaoh got his spiritual strength to rule from Satan's marine kingdom. The Vatican is referred to as the Holy See (Holy Sea) the center for marine kingdom divination which is what the word 'Vatican' means, the center of divination. The Pope is one of Satan's most powerful sorcerers, he is the false prophet who will give his power to the antichrist and a great enemy to the church as well as an enemy to the true children of Israel.

CHAPTER SIX

Money and The Marine Kingdom

When one is talking about this world's money, one is dealing with the marine kingdom. Money is discussed using marine kingdom terminology. This is crucial because money is not taught in schools and yet money is needed for everyday life. Financial terminology with similarities to water include but are not limited to:

- Financial liquidity (how quickly you can get your hands on your cash)
- Liquid assets (An asset that can be converted into cash in a short time)
- Cash flow (the movement of money)
- Bank (The land alongside a river or a lake or a financial institution that is licensed to deal with money and its substitutes by accepting time and demand deposits, making loans, and investing securities)
- Loan Shark (a moneylender who charges extremely high-interest rates, usually under illegal conditions)

- Float (Money Supply)

- Bank Float (the time it takes to clear the item from the time it was deposited to the time funds were credited to the depositing bank)

- Sink or Swim (a situation in which someone must either succeed on his own or fail on his own).

- Sale (the exchange of a commodity for money) but a sale on a ship harnesses the wind in order to propel the ship.

- Currency (a system of money in general use) base word current meaning a body of water or air moving in a definite direction.

- Revenue stream (a source of revenue of a company or organization)

- Frozen assets (assets which are held until debts are paid)

- Volume (In Capital markets, volume is the amount of a security that was traded during a given period of time.

- Volatility (liability to change quickly and surprisingly, especially for the worse) also can be defined as the tendency of a substance to evaporate at normal temperatures. Markets, like substances, can be volatile. etc.

The ancient Egyptian eagle is utilized by nations such as the United States, which carry the same spirit.

Fair Use (used for the purpose of education) The Egyptian eagle or Phoenix.

Then compare it to the symbol on U.S. currency:

Fair use (used for the purpose of education) American eagle or Phoenix.

In the image of the U.S. dollar bill eagle, the claws can be seen holding 13 arrows in one claw, symbolizing the 13 bloodlines which rule the world. The history books will tell you that the number 13 connotes the 13 original colonies, but we know better. The arrows connote military might. The left-hand claw holds an olive branch with 13 leaves also symbolizing the 13 families, while the leaves connote political inclinations of peace (supposedly). Above the eagle's head are 13 stars in the shape of a hexagram. We already know that the number 13 represents the 13 satanic bloodlines which rule the world. The hexagram is the most powerful symbol in sorcery.

This hexagram star is spoken of in Amos 5:26

"But ye have borne the tabernacle of your Moloch and Chiun, your images, the STAR of your God, which ye made unto yourselves."

Fair use (used for educational purposes)

The star is deceitfully called the "star of David," but that is a lie! It is the star of Moloch according to the word of God. The hexagram is a symbol of sigil magic. The U.S. dollar is filled with sigil magic symbolism. The sigil magic hexagram is a pictorial signature of a demon or fallen angel. It is used in the highest levels of sorcery in order to conjure this evil spirit. Sigil magic has the power to compel one to behave in a manner which is not in their own best interest. The presence of money can often induce pride and a wasteful, self-indulging vanity. After it is drawn on the ground, witches and/or wizards (or worshipful masters, or Freemasons, satanic priests, catholic priests, Hindu priests, Mormon priests, etc.) recite incantations and conjure fallen angels, principalities, powers, rulers of the darkness of this world and spiritual wickedness in high places. Is it any wonder that the subject of money is not taught in schools? This in depth teaching has not been taught in mainstream Christian churches also. Will such a message ever empower TBN viewers? How about GodTV, Daystar, or CBN for that matter? There are many reasons these truths are hidden from view by those who have the power to broadcast the truth to great numbers, but what is important is that the Holy Spirit is revealing this truth to His servants and His servants are delivering it to the true children of God.

"Therefore rejoice, ye heavens, and ye that dwell in them. Woe to the inhabiters of the earth and of the sea! for the devil is come down unto you, having great wrath because he knoweth that he hath but a short time." Revelation 12:12 KJV

Ephesians 6:12 gives more profound insight into the entities which rule this world.

"For we wrestle not against flesh and blood, but against principalities, against powers, against the rulers of the darkness of this world, against spiritual wickedness in high places."

These entities work closely with the 13 Satanic bloodlines which control global banking and the banks work closely with multinational corporations which in turn work closely with governments which in turn tax hardworking employed citizens and give tax breaks to corporations which work closely with banks which again are owned by the satanic bloodlines, e.g. the house of Rothschild.

"The rich rule over the poor, and the borrower is servant to the lender."Proverbs 22:7

The privately owned Federal Reserve Bank in the United States (which is not Federal, neither does it have any gold reserves) prints and lends currency to the U.S. government and its citizens as well as foreigners. Every dollar printed must be repaid with interest. If the borrower is servant to the lender, then clearly the U.S. government is not the servant of the citizens of America but is servant to the lender, the 13 banking families and their proxies which rule the world through banking.

Egypt ruled over and enslaved the Hebrew children of Israel for 400 years. Then God raised up Prophet Moses in order to deliver them. God instructed Moses to meet Pharaoh by the river early in the morning. Exodus 7:15

> *"Get thee unto Pharaoh in the morning; lo, he goeth out unto the water; and thou shalt stand by the river's brink against he come; and the rod which was turned into a serpent shalt thou carry in thine hand."*

Pharaoh was not going to the river early in the morning to bathe. He had a huge palace with rooms where even his servants could bathe. Pharaoh was going to the riverside to call upon the water spirits to covenant himself further and draw strength from the marine kingdom. He would not go there without a sacrificial offering. Pharaoh's power to rule over the children of God came from Satan's marine kingdom.

> *"The thing that has been, it is that which shall be, and that which is done is that which shall be done; and*

there is no new thing under the sun." Ecclesiastes 1:9

Lucifer's Altar

Is today's modern-day slavery just a repeat of that which has been?

Are God's children being enslaved by Egypt again?

African currencies are some of the weakest currencies in the world, and yet Africa has more gold and natural resources than the whole world combined. It is not the west that offers aid to Africa, it is Africa which offers aid to the west.

Natural resources from Africa prop up and bolster western economies, yet Africa is filled with poor and disenfranchised men, women and children. The vengeance of God written about in Obadiah against Edom is justifiable. Soon the plundering of Jacob and the children of God will end.

Fair use (used for the purposes of education)

The world buys their crude oil in U.S. dollars. This makes the U.S. dollar the base currency of the world. The whole world offers their goods and services in exchange for the dollar. This puts the dollar in a unique position of power over all other currencies. One U.S. dollar is roughly Kshs 100 shillings. Kenya, like other countries, buys its oil in U.S. dollars.

The pyramid pictured on the dollar bill is the Egyptian pyramid. It is not and has never been a symbol of American patriotism. The pyramid is the throne and altar of Lucifer. The Egyptians possessed the secrets given to them from Satan and his fallen angels. They used this power to enslave the Hebrew children of Israel. Do you see the parallels between then and now? The 13 families which possess this satanic marine kingdom power use it to plunder the world and push it towards a New World Order.

Above the pyramid on the dollar bill are the Latin words "annuit coeptis" meaning "he is pleased with our progress thus far" while the Latin words below the pyramid "Novus Ordo Seclorum" mean New Secular World Order. So, the entire symbol signifies that Lucifer is pleased with the progress of the builders of the new secular (Godless) order thus far. One must prayerfully take into account that business and the realm of the spirit go hand in hand. The kingdom of darkness has been at the forefront of big business for thousands of years. Anyone who is not born again, and is simply working for money, is actually serving Lucifer by default.

Jesus made this issue very clear:

> *"He who is not with Me is against Me; and he who does not gather with Me scatters."Matthew 12:30*

So, billions of people who are not born again but are just going through the daily grind of going to work, so they can get money and come back home to pay bills are actually serving Lucifer and helping him build his new digital totalitarian world order. This is a system of slavery, but Satan's system has always been a system of slavery, and there is nothing new about that.

Slavery has always been big business. After Moses led the children of Israel out of Egypt by the power of God, he prophesied to them about their future if they obeyed the commandments of God, as well as the consequences of disobedience. Deuteronomy 28 speaks of the blessings of obedience from verse 1 to 14. But from verse 15 all the way through to verse 68 are a long list of prophetic curses. One of the many curses was as follows:

> *"The LORD shall bring a nation against thee from far, from the end of the earth, as swift as the eagle flieth; a nation whose tongue thou shalt not understand;" (Deuteronomy 28:49)*

This is clearly Edom or America, whose symbol (like Rome) is the eagle. The English language was as foreign to the Hebrew as any other language he had never heard, and America was definitely on the other side of the earth from where Israel had been scattered. Then Deuteronomy 28:68 hits the nail on the head as one of the most powerful fulfillments of bible prophecy ever written:

"And the Lord shall bring thee into Egypt AGAIN with ships, by the way, whereof I spoke unto thee, thou shalt see it no more again: and there ye shall be SOLD unto your enemies for bondmen and bondwomen, and no man shall buy you."

(Hebrew slaves in slave ship, Deuteronomy 28:68)

This prophecy foretells the transatlantic slave trade in the most precise detail. The Hebrews did reject Jesus Christ and did hand him over to be crucified by Pilate. Then in AD 70, Rome, led by the Roman general Titus, invaded Israel from the north and crushed Jerusalem with an iron fist just as Jesus had prophesied to his disciples before his death and resurrection in 33 AD

> *"And Jesus said to him, "Do you see these great buildings? Not one stone will be left upon another which will not be torn down." Mark 13:2*

Sure enough, when Rome invaded Jerusalem from the north, the inhabitants were pushed towards the south. The only land south of Israel is Egypt or Africa. The children of Israel were scattered, just as the bible prophesied they would be. Then around 1611 (roughly 400 years ago) the transatlantic slave trade began and the children of Israel were brought back to spiritual "Egypt" (America) AGAIN in slave ships just as Moses prophesied in Deuteronomy 28:68.

INSPECTION AND SALE OF A NEGRO

(Fair Use, Educational purposes) Hebrews being sold to their enemies Deuteronomy 28:68 described in perfect detail.

The Hebrews were scattered all over Africa and from Africa's slave coasts all over the world to serve their enemies, just as the Bible prophesied. Arabs also played a huge role in African slavery. Any African who refused to convert to Islam was made a slave. As a result, many Africans became Muslims in an effort to avoid slavery. Those who did not convert were enslaved. All over Africa, European nations like Britain, France, Germany and Belgium colonized African countries taking the best farmland, exploiting the indigenous populations and taking the national resources back to their home countries. Another fulfillment of Deuteronomy 28:43:

"The stranger that is within thee shall get up above thee very high; and thou shalt come down very low."

How is it that a few Europeans could rule over, enslave, subjugate and exploit millions of Africans in their own homeland throughout the entire continent of Africa if it were not the fulfillment of Deuteronomy 28:43. Till this day Congo is still one of the wealthiest countries in the world in terms of natural resources including gold, coltan, platinum, uranium, copper, titanium, bauxite etc., blessings from God which do not seem to be a blessing to the people of Congo but are more like a curse since the local military fights over these resources on behalf of westerners and the inhabitants are robbed of everything including their peace.

Western governments and corporations send their emissaries to systematically destabilize the wealthiest African nations and exploit their natural resources. Then, backed by huge P.R. campaigns, the western world is misled to believe that Africa is poor and dying and in great need of western assistance. So-called charities like OXFAM, UNICEF, RED CROSS, LIFE AID and many other organizations which continuously run multimillion dollar advertising campaigns depicting charity work, sustain an impoverished global image of Africa. All the while collecting monies from innocent westerners who believe they are helping out but are only keeping the ruthless cycle of the exploitation of Africa by the west going. Most of the money given to these "charities" is used by the charities themselves for salaries, bonuses, allowances, insurance and more money is poured into advertising to keep the money flowing. By the time operating expenses are covered, only pennies are left. While one western hand gives "charity" under the flashing lights of cameras, the other hand takes and exploits natural resources wholesale.

Not much has changed since the transatlantic slave trade began around the year 1611. The following 400 years of slavery in the United States of America bolstered America's economy to become the most powerful economy in the world. Edom was now exploiting the blessing on Jacob's life (Isaac blessed Jacob in Genesis 27:28-29) while taking advantage of the prophesied curses upon Jacob if he disobeyed the commandments of God (Deuteronomy 28:15-68) which they did disobey. As the transatlantic slave trade began, many Hebrews had migrated to West Africa and continued procreating and migrating throughout Africa and scattered and became known as the Bantu tribes. Many had strayed from the oracles of righteousness inscribed in the Torah and converted to Islam. Others, whose ancestors had rejected Christ, delved deep into witchcraft. Indeed, until this day, witchcraft has stretched across the African continent and impoverished the inhabitants of the wealthiest continent on the face of the earth. Ecclesiastes 11:1,2 says,

> *"There is an evil which I have seen under the sun, and it is common among men: A man to whom God hath given riches, wealth, and honor, so that he wanted nothing for his soul of all that he desired, yet God giveth him not power to eat thereof, but a stranger eateth it: this is vanity, and it is an evil disease."*

Just before the industrial revolution, cotton was the biggest business in the world and America was at the forefront of cotton exports to Europe and the rest of the world. Hebrew slaves across the American south were paid nothing in exchange for their hard labor in the sweltering hot sun. This was work their white masters could never do, since the hot sun would have overwhelmed them in the fields. Then came the invention of the cotton gin in 1793. The cotton gin revolutionized the cotton industry in the United States, but also led to the growth of slavery in the American south as the demand for cotton labor increased dramatically. The invention also laid the groundwork for the culmination of the industrial revolution. Many also believe that the cotton gin invention was an inadvertent contributing factor to the outbreak of the American Civil War, since slavery brought great wealth to slave owners across the south. The primary beneficiaries of free black Hebrew slave labor were the bankers of their times, many of whom were so-called "Jews.". Jews were so involved with slavery that the buying and selling of Hebrew slaves was suspended during Jewish holidays. Jews owned thc huge, expensive shipping vessels (which were cash flow assets) and were the primary bankers in that time, just as they are today.

The most powerful Jewish banks got their early head start during the slave trade, and subsequent years of free slave labor put Jewish banks far ahead of other banks and provided the foundation for what would later become the New York Stock Exchange on Wall Street.

> *"I know thy works, and tribulation, and poverty, (but thou art rich) and I know the blasphemy of them which say they are Jews, and are not, but are the synagogue of Satan." (Revelation 2:9)*

Fair Use (used for educational purposes)

Ashkenazi "Jews" are Khazarian (Eastern European) converts to Judaism. They were a Turkic people who established a major commercial empire around the 6th century, covering the southeastern section of modern European Russia. They were and are a commercially brilliant people. They are brilliant in banking, and other areas of financial management.

They had always been pagans as far as their spiritual backgrounds were concerned. Their gods never included the God of the Hebrews. They converted to Judaism around the 9th and 10th centuries. It is believed that they did so in order to avoid converting to Christianity and submitting themselves to the Pope of Rome, and to avoid converting to Islam and submitting themselves to the Caliph in Baghdad. Prior to that time, they had never been "Hebrews." Please feel free to investigate and research this information for yourself. You can begin by reading "The 13th tribe: The Khazar Empire and Its Heritage" by Arthur Koestler, himself a "Jew" who admits that the "Jews" are not the descendants of the Hebrews of antiquity but from Khazars, a Turkic people. This book was published in 1976. I urge any genuine Christian to investigate this matter with a clean heart. The Holy Spirit will lead you into all truth. This truth will reveal the fact that the 1948 occupation of Palestine was not an act of God, but rather an act of Rothschild, the satanic banking family which still controls and owns the central banks of the world. This information can be investigated simply by reading about "The Balfour Declaration," and other facts of history, including how World War Two helped to bring about Jewish Zionist state in Palestine.

Meanwhile, the church in the west is convinced that the "Jews" were brought back "on eagle's wings," by the "hand of God" and yet, the elaborate plot can be understood simply by reading about it. The "Jews" have definitely duped the church. And since "Jews" run media houses, they are able to cover the truth and prevent those who do not dig deep to find the truth from finding out what is happening. Modern day Israel is not the historical Israel of antiquity. It is a secular state, where gay pride parades in Tel Aviv are commonplace. This cover up is one of the biggest deceptions in the western church today. The fact that America (and many other nations) enslaved the true children of Israel (who are black) for 400 years is a shocking truth. To make it worse, this was the second time they had been enslaved.

> *"And the LORD shall bring thee into Egypt AGAIN with ships, by the way, whereof I spake unto thee, thou shalt see it no more again: and there ye shall be sold unto your enemies for bondmen and bondwomen, and no man shall buy you." (Deuteronomy 28:68)*

America is spiritual Egypt. That may be difficult for you to believe, but have another look at the U.S. one-dollar bill.

Why would there be an Egyptian pyramid on American currency if Egypt had nothing to do with America? When Erica, my wife, went to hell, she saw Satan (Lucifer) seated on his throne on top of a pyramid. The only source of light in that place was the dull moonlight which emanated from behind his throne through an eye shaped hole. She speaks candidly about her experience in hell and what she saw as she served Satan for seven years face to face in her book series 'Erica Part One, Seven Years in Hell.' (The Ebook is available on Amazon Kindle, while the actual book may be obtained by calling one of the numbers on the back of this publication or emailing our ministry through the email provided on the back of this book.) It was Satan who was operating through Pharaoh. When you sell your soul to the devil, the devil takes over your body and soul.

Jesus knew this and therefore asked:

> *"For what is a man profited, if he shall gain the whole world, and lose his own soul? or what shall a man give in exchange for his soul?" (Matthew 16:26)*

Your soul is your mind, your will and your emotions. Pharaoh had sold his soul (his mind, his will and his emotions) to the devil for money, power and fame, just like many Freemasons and politicians do today.

Egypt enslaved the Hebrew children of Israel the first time because they forgot their God and lost their true identity. The moment you forget who you are, you become a slave. Lack of identity is the same as slavery. The truth is that the moment the Hebrews turned their backs on Jesus Christ in 33 AD, they lost their identity. As soon as you lose your identity, you become a slave.

> *"Jesus answered them, "Most certainly I tell you, everyone who commits sin is the bondservant of sin."* (John 8:34)

As soon as you turn away from God, you become a slave of sin. The Hebrews became slaves of sin for an additional 400 years for the 2nd time. This is why Jesus cried out, saying;

> *"Oh, Jerusalem, Jerusalem, the city that kills the prophets and stones those sent to her! How often I wanted to gather your children together, just as a hen gathers her brood under her wings, and you would not have it! Behold, your house is left to you desolate; and I say to you, you will not see Me until the time comes when you say, 'BLESSED IS HE WHO COMES IN THE NAME OF THE LORD!"* (Luke 13:34-35)

Jesus knew that if they turned away from him, they would become the servants of sin, slaves.

This is why when Jesus was being led away to be crucified and the women were weeping, Jesus said this,

> *"And following Him was a large crowd of the people, and of women, who were mourning and lamenting Him. But Jesus turning to them said, "Daughters of Jerusalem, stop weeping for Me, but weep for yourselves and for your children."For behold, the days are coming when they will say, 'Blessed are the barren, and the wombs that never bore, and the*

breaststhat never nursed.' "Then they will begin TO SAY TO THE MOUNTAINS, 'FALL ON US,' AND TO THE HILLS, 'COVER US.' (Luke 23:27-30)

Jesus' words were so true. When the slave trade was at its height, bringing children into the world was a miserable thing because the quality of life was guaranteed to be miserable for the slave child. The truth is that the New World Order is built on the back of Hebrew and Gentile disobedience to God. All who reject Christ will play their role in building Satan's New World Order, simply by not serving God. There are only two agendas on the face of the entire earth. They are:

1. The salvation of mankind and

2. The destruction of mankind

All human economic activity falls under either one of these two categories. You will align yourself along one of these two agendas because money is made by providing assistance. So, either you will provide assistance for the salvation of mankind or you will provide assistance for mankind's destruction. Either way, you will provide assistance in exchange for money. Money is the byproduct of assistance.

The more assistance you can provide, the more money you can make. Those who are saved and serving the Lord, provide assistance for the salvation of mankind. Some provide assistance simply by giving their money for the spread of the gospel of the Kingdom of God. Others are in part-time ministry and others in full-time ministry. But those who do not serve Jesus, by default, are serving Lucifer. Unfortunately, many serve him innocently, without knowing. Jesus said,

> "He who is not with Me is against Me; and he who does not gather with Me, scatters." (Luke 11:23)

> *" But when he, the Spirit of truth, comes, he will guide you into all the truth. He will not speak on his own; he will speak only what he hears, and he will tell you what is yet to come." (John 16:13)*

God spoke through the prophet Ezekiel. He prophesied concerning the downfall of Satan's financial system, his black market and his banking system.

> *"Thy riches, and thy fairs, thy merchandise, thy mariners, and thy pilots, thy calkers, and the occupiers of thy merchandise, and all thy men of war, that are in thee, and in all thy company, which is in the midst of thee, shall fall into the midst of the seas in the day of thy ruin. (Ezekiel 27:27) Verses 33-34 declare,*

> *"When thy wares went forth out of the seas, thou filledst many people; thou didst enrich the kings*

of the earth with the multitude of thy riches and of thy merchandise. In the time when thou shalt be broken by the seas in the depths of the waters, thy merchandise and all thy company in the midst of thee shall fall."

If one is going to understand the role evil business has played in the building of Satan's New World Order, one must also understand the destructive power of compromise. The word 'merchant' spoken of in Ezekiel 27 is often understood to simply mean 'business person.' But this definition does not paint the true picture of what a 'merchant' is according to the bible.

"And the light of a candle shall shine no more at all in you; and the voice of the bridegroom and of the bride shall be heard no more at all in you: for your merchants were the great men of the earth; for by your sorceries were all nations deceived." (Revelation 18:23)

The word merchant is made up of the prefix "mer" which means 'pertaining to water or the love of water or sea' while the word "chant" means to recite or sing words to a rhythm for the purpose of incantation used to raise energy or induce a trance-like state. A 'mer-maid' is a water maid or lady of the sea etc.

So a mer-chant is a water enchanter or water spirit conjurer, while merchandise are the commodities which the merchant sells to unsuspecting customers. Merchants sell their souls to the marine kingdom in exchange for money, power and fame. The same money, power and fame Satan offered Jesus in Luke 4:6,7.

> "And the devil said unto him, all this power will I give thee, and the glory of them: for that is delivered unto me; and to whomsoever I will I give it. If thou therefore wilt worship me, all shall be thine."

Sorcery and business have been closely intertwined for centuries. Those who dominated business did so in conjunction with the covenants they entered into with the marine kingdom. It may be difficult to believe, but most of the major brand names we have come to know and patronize may be some of hell's biggest industries. This is why you should pray over everything you buy and over everything you own. No wonder the word says;

> "Love not the world, neither the things that are in the world. If any man loves the world, the love of the Father is not in him." (1 John 2:15)

So Pharaoh was little more than a merchant for the marine kingdom. The marine kingdom is a great enemy of the church.

Since man's body is 70% water, the influence of the marine kingdom cannot be ignored. But God promises Abraham in Genesis 22:17,

> "Indeed I will greatly bless you, and I will greatly multiply your seed as the stars of the heavens and as the sand which is on the seashore; and your seed shall possess the gate of their enemies."

There is more good news! Galatians 3:29 (NIV) says,

> "If you belong to Christ, then you are Abraham's seed, and heirs according to the promise."

If Africa and the Christian world is going to rise from the ashes of servitude and slavery to Edom, and take their place as the sons of God, and if the true children of Israel are going to defeat Pharaoh and his system of slavery, they must study their enemy, learn their true identities in Christ and rise to the occasion.

If one is going to earn money, does it not make sense to understand the nature and the purpose of the thing one is earning? We spend years in school so that we can earn money and provide for our families by providing goods and services in society. But we spend no time studying money. You can have the power to control your future if you have the proper financial information. The children of God should not work for money, but money should work for them. Sadly, the subject of money is not taught in schools. It is up to the church to correct this anomaly.

Unfortunately for most poor African's or citizens of 3rd world countries and even developed country's citizens, access to capital is oftentimes reserved for the rich. The system is designed to benefit the few at the expense of the many. It will occasionally allow a new face to rise through the ranks to perpetuate the idea that success for all in a capitalist system is possible. This serves two purposes.

1. It quells any reason for civilian uprising
2. and It sells the image of the capitalist system as benevolent and welcoming to newcomers. Nothing could be further from the truth. The "new money" only acts as a buffer between the wealthy minority and the masses in poverty. Celebrities are created for this purpose. To entertain and keep the masses busy with nonsense of little to no real value. The celebrities are often highly paid witches themselves, being used by the synagogue of Satan to curse the masses and keep them under control. If they are not full blown witches they will be what are called "blind witches," which are just low level slaves who think they're being promoted for

their talent and are so deceived that they actually feel lucky to be in their positions!

In the days of the empire of Rome, the colosseum was used to amuse the mobs. They would pack the stadium and watch as Christians were devoured by lions and other wild animals. During that time a Christian was viewed as the most unfortunate kind of person the world had ever seen. They were slaughtered in front of thousands of screaming fans for entertainment. Their heads would roll on the ground and be kicked around by gladiators. This is the evil origin of many so-called sports. The role that sports plays in pulling people away from God and his word today cannot be ignored. Men pack sports bars to watch the game and can tell you the names of all the players but cannot recite John 3:16. Is entertainment really a friend of the people or is it an enemy in disguise sent to distract the masses from what really matters? Raising our families in God fearing homes and being examples of righteousness, preaching the Kingdom of God to a dark and dying world is what we should be focused on. But if both parents are in the office working for money while the children are being raised by Walt Disney witchcraft cartoons and Hollywood movies and the parents bewitched by the same system of entertainment, then the future of a luciferian New World Order is not only very possible, it is extremely likely and the bible, like as other times, has foretold it.

There is good news though. Financial education and the teaching of financial freedom in the body of Christ is mainly for the purpose of allowing parents and future parents to be with their children and give them the attention they need while still earning a great living. The history of money and its connection to slavery and Egypt outlined in this book is not for the purpose of inciting hatred or anger. Rather on the contrary, it is for the purpose of opening the eyes of the readers to the sins of the world and the dire need for real preachers, teachers, evangelists, pastors, prophets and apostles who really know what happened, what is happening and what is going to happen, so as to empower the next generation. We are living in the last days. Preparing now for what is coming tomorrow is a definition of wisdom.

Before the year 1971, the United States dollar was worth 1/35th of an ounce of gold. In other words, one dollar was only printed if there was 1/35th of an ounce of gold in the banking reserves to back it. A dollar was a receipt for a piece of gold being held by the bank. By taking the U.S. dollar off of the gold standard, president Richard Nixon devalued the dollar. It is no longer backed by gold but by the good faith of the United States treasury department. In 1971 an ounce of gold was roughly $43 USD. This was before Nixon took the dollar off of the gold standard. Today the same ounce of gold is about $1,276.86 USD (gold prices fluctuate from day to day depending on supply & demand factors and market sentiment). This shows a devaluation of the US dollar. This devaluation seems to be continuing. As at Wednesday, May 22, 2019

The U.S. rate of inflation is at 2% for the 12 months ended April 2019. Inflation is the devaluation of a nation's currency due to quantitative easing which is simply an increase in the money supply. In other words, if you had $1,000,000USD in the bank on May 22nd, 2018, by May 22nd, 2019, your $1,000,000USD would still be in the bank but with a 2% loss of value. This is why the rich do not like to save cash money in the bank. Saving cash in the bank results in loss of cash value due to inflation. The rich keep their money moving, or invest in real estate or commodities like gold so as inflation rises, the price of gold rises with it and so does the amount of money they have as a direct result. But before investing in gold or any other commodity, it is absolutely critical that you make a more important investment, that is the investment you make in your own mind. In other words, your financial situation will not change until you do. The change in your pocket comes as a direct result of the change in your mind. So the initial acquisition of Capital is not the first investment check (cheque) you receive. It is the initial decision you make to increase your financial knowledge base. If the dollar is gradually losing value, how long will it take before it completely collapses? What can you do to prepare for this seeming inevitability? The book of revelation gives us a reliable glimpse into the future. The coming New World Order leader will force everyone to receive a mark on their hand or their forehead and without this "mark," you will not be able to buy or sell.

> "And he causes all, both small and great, rich and poor, free and bond, to receive a mark in their right hand, or in their foreheads: And that no man might buy or sell, save he that had the mark, or the name of the beast, or the number of his name. Here is wisdom. Let him that hath understanding count the number of the beast: for it is the number of a man; and his number is Six hundred threescore and six." (Revelation 13:16)

The future of financial transactions will be digital. Already VISA, MASTERCARD and other credit cards are digitally based with microchips embedded in the cards. As we have already seen, 97% of all currency is digital. Only 3% is in actual cash or coins. In Kenya the M-Pesa system makes it possible to send and receive money digitally, directly from your bank account to your smart phone and then from your phone back to your bank account or to other cell phone numbers. The bible already foretold over 2,000 years ago that the digital financial age would come and now we are right at the precipice of a New World Order (NWO). I believe this NWO has been in the workings by evil leaders and unsuspecting followers for thousands of years. This is the working of the spirit of antichrist.

> "And every spirit that confesseth not that Jesus Christ is come in the flesh is not of God: and this is that spirit of antichrist, whereof ye have heard that it should come; and even now already is it in the world." (1 John 4:3)

The symbol of the star of Moloch inscribed above the eagle's head on the back of the one-dollar bill is the sigil magic (sorcery) signature of the spirit of antichrist.

Fair use (For purposes of education)

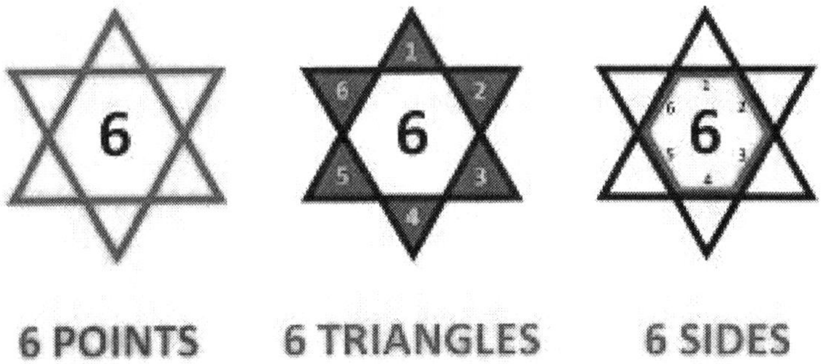

Fair use (for purposes of education) The hexagram is the geometric representation of the spirit of antichrist, it's signature and number is 666.

> "Here is wisdom. Let him who has understanding calculate the number of the beast, for the number is that of a man; and his number is six hundred and sixty-six."

(Revelation 13:18)

Fair Use (Educational purposes) The Star of Moloch, falsely called the "star of David."

The symbol of antichrist, openly emblazoned on the flag of modern day secular Israel.

The bible tells us that 666 is the number of a man. I believe that man is Cain, for he was the first in whom the spirit of antichrist acted. The antichrist spirit is a murderous, violent, killing, jealous, spirit.

> *"And the LORD said unto him, therefore whosoever slayeth Cain, vengeance shall be taken on him sevenfold. And the LORD set a mark upon Cain, lest any finding him should kill him." (Genesis 4:15)*

The Lord put a mark on Cain (the first antichrist). Could this mark be similar to the mark of the beast? The beast in revelation 13 is the financial system. Humanity is now headed in a direction, in the foreseeable future, where human beings will be forced to receive DNA altering microchips containing identification information, financial information, biological (medical records) information and your location. Anyone who takes this mark will no longer be a part of the human family. They will have sold their soul to Lucifer. In exchange they are given access to the financial system through the mark. Global Wi-Fi will be available by then. Anyone who has the mark but proves to be against the system will have their "chip" turned off remotely. The power of life and death may be in that chip. The world leaders endorse and support the taking of the mark, religious leaders, celebrities, superstars, politicians, and therefore the vast majority of the world will take this mark. Taking this mark is covenanting yourself with Lucifer. Remember Jesus words in Luke 21:19

> *"In your patience, possess ye your souls."*

Many believe that the church will have been raptured by then, but the word "rapture" does not appear in the bible. Furthermore, the only thing we know about the coming of the Lord is that:

> *"But of that day and hour knoweth no man, no, not the angels of heaven, but my Father only." (Matthew 24:36)*

It is better to be prepared for the tribulation, and then be taken away and not need it, than to not be prepared for the tribulation, expecting to disappear, and be found unprepared. Those who prepare for hard times, during the good times, will not have hard times. Knowing what is going to happen before it happens can help you position yourself advantageously. The essence of business is foresight. The word 'profit' (an increase in return on investment) and 'prophet' (one who sees the past, present and future) are not closely related by accident. The bible speaks of perilous times coming. It would behoove us to be prepared.

In Kenya, I believe this New World Order has been dubbed "Vision 2030." Its promotion is covered with the veneer of politically correct key words such as "sustainable development" and "economic growth." If Kenya's government (and those who control Kenya's government) wanted real economic growth for Kenyan citizens, schools would teach on financial intelligence and concentrate on the study of money, its origins and the nature of capitalism in high schools and Universities. The vision 2030 wording is given to Kenya's leaders by the owners of capitalism. The "leaders" then repeat it in their speeches on television for public consumption.

The spirit of Pharaoh will never allow the Hebrew children of God to enjoy their inheritance in the earth. This is why God had to intervene then, and He will have to intervene again. The spirit of white supremacy, is the same spirit of Pharaoh. In the 1960s in America it was called Jim Crow. Across Africa throughout the colonial era it was called colonialism. The picture of a white Jesus is part of the public relations campaign of the spirit of white supremacy. The white supremacy spirit is an antichrist spirit. This spirit has its global base in the Vatican. The white Pope claiming to be the "vicar of Christ," or 'instead of Christ,' is an enemy of God and the body of Christ. Exposing white supremacy is not about hating people. Sharing the love of Christ is the greatest act of love one can possibly offer any race. Identifying who the Hebrews are and who they are not, is not an act of hatred or racism. Speaking truth is always an act of love. The church is the ground and pillar of truth.

> *"But if I tarry long, that thou mayest know how thou oughtest to behave thyself in the house of God, which is the church of the living God, the pillar and ground of the truth." (1 Timothy 3:15)*

I personally wish that all races would receive Jesus Christ. That is the essence of spreading love to all mankind.

Chapter Seven

The Heart Of God

"Ye are bought with a price; be not ye the servants of men." 1 Corinthians 7:23 KJV

Anyone who does not understand the unjust nature of the financial system and how to make the necessary adjustments will definitely find themselves being a slave of the same in one way or another whether you are a Christian or not. There are ways out of the economic system of oppression but one must know about these ways.

"...through knowledge shall the just be delivered. (Proverbs 11:9 KJV)

Otherwise they will be stuck in the labyrinth of the financial world without a roadmap. That is a recipe for financial ruin. We have already covered how purchasing of assets (income generators) can lift a person out of the cycle of poverty and can project them into the stratosphere of economic stability. This wisdom does not come from your favorite motivational speaker or some financial guru but has its origin in Heaven and was expressed in writing by King Solomon in the fourteenth chapter of the book of Proverbs the fourth verse:

> *"Where no oxen are, the crib is clean: but much increase is by the strength of the ox."(Proverbs 14:4 KJV)*

Oxen in this case are assets or income generators. We observed how the poor generally lack income generators. They, themselves, are the income generators. So if they get sick, their income stops. We saw how the educational system is designed to keep you oblivious of income generators and how they prefer that you actually be the income generator with jobs being offered to employees with various skill sets and corresponding compensation packages which will never be enough to leave anything but debt behind for your children, let alone your children's children.

> *"A good man leaveth an inheritance to his children's children: and the wealth of the sinner is laid up for the just." (Proverbs 13:22 KJV)*

We sat in disbelief at the utter arrogance and complete disdain for justice and fairness which was perpetrated by Wall Street on the entire world as some of the biggest financial culprits in the world received bailouts worth billions of dollars of taxpayers money while the common man received no bail out at all. Then, to add insult to injury, the CEOs awarded themselves huge multimillion dollar bonuses while the financial institutions they ran either went out of business or were bailed out with tax payers blood sweat and tears. I have chosen to remind you of these things so that you understand that not only is the system rigged to enrich the few at the expense of the many, but anyone who does not serve Jesus Christ is a slave of this same system by default.

> *"He that is not with me is against me; and he that gathereth not with me scattereth abroad."(Matthew 12:30 KJV)*

Financial freedom for Christians is extremely important. Without it, you will be an economic slave, trading your time in exchange for just enough money to travel to and from work every day, enough not to starve to death and enjoy some leisure time with your friends on the weekends. Then start the whole process over again on Monday.

This strenuous cycle takes a toll on the family and provides inroads for the enemy to spend more time with your children than you do. By the time you make it back home after spending all that time stuck in traffic, you're exhausted. You sit down and have a meal, take a shower and jump in bed and that's only if you don't fall asleep on the couch!

All that being said, this book would be incomplete without a chapter dealing specifically with how Christians and any decent human being should view the poor and how that view can either make them or break them in life. There are quite a few scriptures dealing with how God views the poor and what He expects to see in human beings who at the very least understand the basic concept of justice and judgement.

> *"For I know him, that he will command his children and his household after him, and they shall keep the way of the Lord, to do justice and judgment; that the Lord may bring upon Abraham that which he hath spoken of him." (Genesis 18:19 KJV)*

God has called all of His children into the office of king and priest.

> *"And hath made us kings and priests unto God and his Father; to him be glory and dominion for ever and ever. Amen. (Revelation 1:6 KJV)*

God has already provided every blessing you will ever need on the earth:

> *"Blessed be the God and Father of our Lord Jesus Christ, who hath blessed us with all spiritual blessings in heavenly places in Christ:" (Ephesians 1:3 KJV)*

The issue is that most Christians don't understand how to obtain that which has already been provided. There is an old saying that goes:

"When the student is ready, the teacher appears."

Whether this was Buddha or some other person who said it is besides the point. The point to be understood is that when man is ready for his inheritance, there are certain things he will do which prove that he is ready to receive his inheritance. Those things which he will do are a function of his understanding of spiritual concepts which cause physical things to happen simply by obeying principles which have long been established. This is what Paul the apostle meant in Galatians chapter four from verse one to verse three:

> *"Now I say, That the heir, as long as he is a child, differeth nothing from a servant, though he be lord of all; But is under tutors and governors until the time appointed of the father. Even so we, when we were children, were in bondage under the elements of the world:" (Galatians 4:1-3 KJV)*

"When the prince becomes a king, he receives his kingdom."

-Timsimon Kimani

When God sent us into the world, and He made sure that we all knew that we arrived here naked, innocent and ignorant. God also placed everything we would ever need in this world here, long before we arrived. Everything we need to finish our course in this world must be obtained by faith. Faith comes by hearing God's word:

> *"So then faith cometh by hearing, and hearing by the word of God." (Romans 10:17 KJV)*

It is only after you realize who you are in Christ and what God has ordained for you that you begin to possess a mindset that produces the kind of life that God desired for you to have before the foundation of the world.

> *"For we are his workmanship, created in Christ Jesus unto good works, which God hath before ordained that we should walk in them." (Ephesians 2:10 KJV)*

Now this glorious life is a function of the wisdom of God which is at work in everyone who has received Jesus Christ. The only thing that can delay or speed up the manifestation of God's plan for your life is your own mindset. Your mindset will either make you or break you!

> *"Let this mind be in you, which was also in Christ Jesus:" (Philippians 2:5 KJV)*

You may or may not believe this but God, in His wisdom, hid your wealth inside of the need of a very poor person who keeps on coming into contact with you but you never realized it. The shocking thing is that the same way people despise and pass a poor person in the street is the same way they pass on opportunities in life.

"The king that faithfully judgeth the poor, his throne shall be established for ever." (Proverbs 29:14 KJV)

The following is a list of scriptures which give a very clear view of how God views the poor and how your views towards them can either make you or break you. The financial centers of the world are filled with brilliant mathematicians all trying to figure out the formula for the creation of massive amounts of wealth. Wall Street hedge fund managers like Ray Dalio of Bridgewater Associates (the world's largest hedge fund) say they have it figured out or at least they think they do. If you looked at how much he's worth you might think he does too (in excess of $20 billion USD) but there's a power he will never tell you that backs his success.

This wealth comes with strings attached. These "strings" are curses which follow their bloodline for three and four generations. We have already established that life is spiritual. That nothing happens physically until it takes place in the realm of the spirit which is the parent realm. The physical world that we see, hear, taste, smell and touch is the offspring realm, a reflection of the spirit realm. Therefore the physical world functions by spiritual laws. These spiritual laws are found in the word of God. I mentioned Ray Dalio but I would not follow the path he has taken if I were you, even though he's a billionaire. This is because he ascribes to transcendental meditation - a practice which he learned from the Beatles who studied the practice in India back in 1968. Ray says that this practice "helps him to think more clearly and creatively when making decisions." This is extremely dangerous and should be avoided by all. This kind of meditation empties the mind and allows evil spirits to enter in and manipulate your life.

> *"But I say, that the things which the Gentiles sacrifice, they sacrifice to devils, and not to God: and I would not that ye should have fellowship with devils." (1 Corinthians 10:20 KJV)*

India is full of idolatry. Many American captains of industry travel there so that they can obtain ideas that will be what the world calls "cutting edge" or "the next big thing." But this is merely fellowshipping with demons in order to receive wealth. They commit idolatry in exchange for this world's goods. There are many very wealthy men who obtained their wealth through entering into covenants with evil spirits who in turn give them temporary wealth. What they don't realize is that the result of sacrificing to idols is that the curses listed in Deuteronomy 28:15-68 will follow your bloodline up to three and four generations later. He bartered his children's future in exchange for this own..."

> *"Thou shalt have no other gods before me. Thou shalt not make unto thee any graven image, or any likeness of any thing that is in heaven above, or that is in the earth beneath, or that is in the water under the earth: Thou shalt not bow down thyself to them, nor serve them: for I the Lord thy God am a jealous God, visiting the iniquity of the fathers upon the children unto the third and fourth generation of them that hate me." (Exodus 20:3-5 KJV)*

The result of sacrificing to idols is that the curses listed in Deuteronomy 28:15-68 will follow your bloodline up to three and four generations later. Ray's great grandchildren won't even know what hit them.

> *"The Lord will smite thee with the botch of Egypt, and with the emerods, and with the scab, and with the itch, whereof thou canst not be healed." (Deuteronomy 28:27 KJV)*

Do you know what emerods are? They are incurable tumors and cancerous cells which form in the body. They have no cure. Now look at how Steve Jobs of Apple passed away. It was well known that Steve Jobs traveled to India just like Ray Dalio did, to fraternize with the deep things of the spirit so that he could be on the cutting edge of what was coming next in the earth. But at what cost? Jobs traveled to India in his teen years and returned to the United States as a Buddhist. He had been seeking to find "his inner self" and seeking to "be enlightened." The result was success in this physical world but the loss of his soul. Jobs died of pancreatic cancer at the age of just fifty six years old. He could have lived far longer than that.

> *"For what shall it profit a man, if he shall gain the whole world, and lose his own soul?" (Mark 8:36 KJV)*

The world will surely miss Steve Jobs and my heartfelt condolences extend to his friends and family. Can you imagine what could have happened if this brilliant mind was used for the cause of the gospel of the Kingdom of God? The good news is that there is a right way to success. Good success exists. It is obtained, not by transcendental meditation, but by meditating in the word of God and doing what it commands us to do.

> *"This book of the law shall not depart out of thy mouth; but thou shalt meditate therein day and night, that thou mayest observe to do according to all that is written therein: for then thou shalt make thy way prosperous, and then thou shalt have good success." (Joshua 1:8 KJV)*

This is the right kind of meditation. It is repeated in Psalms:

> *"Blessed is the man that walketh not in the counsel of the ungodly, nor standeth in the way of sinners, nor sitteth in the seat of the scornful. But his delight is in the law of the Lord; and in his law doth he meditate day and night. And he shall be like a tree planted by the rivers of water, that bringeth forth his fruit in his season; his leaf also shall not wither; and whatsoever he doeth shall prosper." (Psalm 1:1-3 KJV)*

Many pastors and spiritual leaders have come out during the era of the "prosperity gospel," teaching the body of Christ that wealth is obtained by Christians through giving and they are partly correct. The problem is that they twisted the scriptures into meaning that they are the ones who we should sow our seeds to! They told us that the more we give to them the more God would bless us. "The bigger the seed, the bigger the harvest," they shouted from the pulpits around the world. But as time progressed, we realized that they were the only ones getting wealthier while the rest of the church became poorer and poorer. The tithe was taken completely out of context and Malachi chapter three was used to extort rather than exhort. We were told that if we failed to tithe, we were cursed and our finances would deteriorate into oblivion. This doctrine turned the church house into a religious pyramid scheme while simultaneously enriching the pastors. The sad part about all of this is that they never emphasized how God's children really gain access to God's blessings. It was never by sowing financial seeds to the rich pastors and prophets, but by giving to the poor.

> *"...he that giveth to the rich, shall surely come to want." (Proverbs 22:16b KJV)*

The principle is so simple. If you give to the rich, you will activate the law of poverty which will make you poor. Satan knows this, so he created a doctrine which would persuade believers to "sow their seed" to pastors who had everything they needed and more. This activated the law of poverty and brought lack and want upon the believers. This is why they never emphasized giving to the poor, because if you give to the poor, you will activate the law of abundance which will release God's blessings upon your life. These are laws which God has established in the earth before He even created mankind. They have always been there. They will never change. Man can either apply these principles and enjoy the fruits or disobey the principles and endure the results. Either way, the law remains.

> *"There is that scattereth, and yet increaseth; and there is that withholdeth more than is meet, but it tendeth to poverty." (Proverbs 11:24 KJV)*

Malachi chapter three is the scripture which most "spiritual leaders" will use to persuade you to believe that if you fail to tithe you will be cursed. Nothing could be further from the truth. Malachi chapter three is just a continuation of Malachi chapter one and chapter two. In these chapters, God was dealing with the tribe of Levi because it was their duty to receive the tithes from the eleven tribes of Israel and then they would tithe from the tithes into the Lord's storehouse. The tribe of Levi received tithes from the eleven tribes because they had no inheritance among the eleven tribes. Theirs was to serve the Lord in the office of the priesthood.

> *"And I, behold, I have taken your brethren the Levites from among the children of Israel: to you they are given as a gift for the Lord, to do the service of the tabernacle of the congregation." (Numbers 18:6 KJV)*

"All the heave offerings of the holy things, which the children of Israel offer unto the Lord, have I given thee, and thy sons and thy daughters with thee, by a statute for ever: it is a covenant of salt for ever before the Lord unto thee and to thy seed with thee.And the Lord spake unto Aaron, Thou shalt have no inheritance in their land, neither shalt thou have any part among them: I am thy part and thine inheritance among the children of Israel. And, behold, I have given the children of Levi all the tenth in Israel for an inheritance, for their service which they serve, even the service of the tabernacle of the congregation." (Numbers 18:20-21 KJV)

So the tribe of Levi had the official duty of receiving the tithes and the offerings from all of Israel. They were to then tithe from the tithes and store those tithes in the Lord's storehouse.

"And the priest the son of Aaron shall be with the Levites, when the Levites take tithes: and the Levites shall bring up the tithe of the tithes unto the house of our God, to the chambers, into the treasure house." (Nehemiah 10:38 KJV)

So only a Levite may receive tithes according to the word of God. And when the tithes are being received by the Levite, a direct descendant of Aaron must be present. Then the tithes of the tithes (10% of all the tithes collected) are then brought up to the storehouse by the Levites so that there would be meat in God's house.

> *"And the Levite that is within thy gates; thou shalt not forsake him; for he hath no part nor inheritance with thee. At the end of three years thou shalt bring forth all the tithe of thine increase the same year, and shalt lay it up within thy gates: And the Levite, (because he hath no part nor inheritance with thee,) and the stranger, and the fatherless, and the widow, which are within thy gates, shall come, and shall eat and be satisfied; that the Lord thy God may bless thee in all the work of thine hand which thou doest."*
>
> *(Deuteronomy 14:27-29 KJV)*

So as you can see, only a Levite may receive tithes, and he must do it in the presence of a direct descendant of Aaron. Furthermore, the purpose of taking the tithes of the tithes into the storehouse was so that distribution could be made to the widow, the orphan, the stranger and the fatherless in the land. That was the heart of the Father! His desire was that those who had nothing would have a part in the economy of the country and not lose hope in God! Why is this not being taught in churches all over the world? Why won't they explain that In Malachi chapter three, the priests had stopped tithing the tithes into the storehouse and now the widow, the orphan, the stranger and the fatherless in the land had become destitute and were now crying out to God for justice?! So God told the Levites that they were cursed with a curse because His storehouse had been robbed and the robbers were the Levites themselves! These Levites were robbing the whole nation of Israel because God would not bless them until distribution was made to those who were suffering!

"Will a man rob God? Yet ye have robbed me. But ye say, Wherein have we robbed thee?

> *In tithes and offerings. Ye are cursed with a curse: for ye have robbed me, even this whole nation. Bring ye all the tithes into the storehouse, that there may be meat in mine house, and prove me now herewith, saith the Lord of hosts, if I will not open you the windows of heaven, and pour you out a blessing, that there shall not be room enough to receive it."(Malachi 3:8-10 KJV)*

When the Lord said "prove me now herewith, if I will not open the windows of Heaven and pour you out a blessing there shall not be room enough to receive," He was talking about what would happen if they gave to the widow, the stranger, the fatherless and the orphan in the land. He was telling them to test Him in this area and see if He would not bless them beyond their ability to contain the blessing in their houses. They would have to move to a bigger house! The enemy knew there was some confusion here and deliberately took advantage of the lack of a clear cut explanation of Malachi chapter three to create a false doctrine which would bring poverty instead of blessing upon the body of Christ! Even Hebrews chapter seven was misinterpreted or only half read!

> *"And here men that die receive tithes; but there he receiveth them, of whom it is witnessed that he liveth. (Hebrews 7:8 KJV)*

These "spiritual leaders" only quote the eighth verse of Hebrews to persuade the congregation that tithing is for the New Testament but they won't read the previous three verses of the same chapter!

> *"And verily they that are of the sons of Levi, who receive the office of the priesthood, have a commandment to take tithes of the people according to the law, that is, OF THEIR BRETHREN, though they come out of the loins of Abraham:" (Hebrews 7:5 KJV)*

So something should be made very clear - only a Levite can receive tithes and a direct descendant of Aaron must be present while the tithes are being received. Furthermore, only the eleven tribes of Israel are allowed to tithe to the tribe of Levi. If your pastor is not a Levite, he has no business collecting tithes. If you are not of the eleven tribes of Israel, you have no business giving tithes. If you do not give any tithes, YOU ARE NOT CURSED!

> *God's design for New Testament giving, as far as the church is concerned, is written by Paul the Apostle in 2 Corinthians 9:7 KJV. It says, "Every man according as he purposeth in his heart, so let him give; not grudgingly, or of necessity: for God loveth a cheerful giver. (2 Corinthians 9:7 KJV)*

Any doctrine concerning New Testament giving other than what Paul wrote is manipulation and coercion. There are many false prophets which have been sent by the devil to fleece the sheep of God. Jesus warned us:

> *"Beware of false prophets, which come to you in sheep's clothing, but inwardly they are ravening wolves." (Matthew 7:15 KJV)*

> *"But [in those days] false prophets arose among the people, just as there will be false teachers among*

> *you, who will subtly introduce destructive heresies, even denying the Master who bought them, bringing swift destruction on themselves. Many will follow their shameful ways, and because of them the way of truth will be maligned. And in their greed they will exploit you with false arguments and twisted doctrine. Their sentence [of condemnation which God has decreed] from a time long ago is not idle [but is still in force], and their destruction and deepening misery is not asleep [but is on its way]." (2 Peter 2:1-3 AMP)*

The tithe was first mentioned in Genesis 14, where Abraham tithed to Melchizedek after the slaughter of the kings. Abraham tithed one time. Melchizedek did not show up at Abraham's tent every Sunday asking for tithes. Abraham also tithed after God had delivered him from all of his enemies and made him very rich. If you are still paying a landlord rent and still working a job for income, then you have not yet been delivered from your enemies. Abraham tithed a tenth of the spoils of war. Where are your spoils of war?

> *"Now consider how great this man was, unto whom even the patriarch Abraham gave the tenth of the spoils." (Hebrews 7:4 KJV)*

If your pastor tells you to tithe because Abraham the father of faith tithed, then tell your pastor you will do so with the spoils of war after God has delivered you from all of your enemies including your landlord and everyone who demands a piece of that paycheck which you are forced to work so hard for. The second time tithe is mentioned is when Jacob promised to tithe if the Lord brought him back to his father Isaac's house in peace.

> *"And Jacob vowed a vow, saying, If God will be with me, and will keep me in this way that I go, and will give me bread to eat, and raiment to put on, So that I come again to my father's house in peace; then shall the Lord be my God: And this stone, which I have set for a pillar, shall be God's house: and of all that thou shalt give me I will surely give the tenth unto thee." (Genesis 28:20-22 KJV)*

There is no scripture indicating that Isaac ever tithed. We therefore have no reason to believe that he ever did.

The doctrine of tithes and sowing of seeds to men of God is one of the many ways which one can identify a false prophet or at the very least, a confused one. God's financial blessings are not released upon those who give to the rich, but upon those who give to the poor. You may have been a tither and a sower of seed for a long time.

Ask yourself . . .

Have the windows of Heaven opened for you and poured you out a blessing that there was no room enough to receive? Have you been showered with blessings yet? If not, something is terribly wrong. God's word does not lie, but men often do. Don't give up on God just because a false prophet took your money through false doctrine. Instead, simply obey the word of God. Give to the poor, the destitute, the widow, visit the sick in the hospital, clear their bills if they cannot afford to pay it. Do this in the name of the Lord and tell them you are giving to them because your God commanded you to do so. You will see the hand of God multiplying your blessings. And I mean finances. Below is the list of verses which every "spiritual leader" of any church should be emphasizing. Instead, many (not all) are busy lining their own pockets with your tithes and offerings and first fruits and thanksgiving seed, and January seed and Mother's Day seed and Father's Day seed and billy goat seed and every other seed they can possibly come up with. May God give you understanding in these last days.

"Blessed is he that considereth the poor: the Lord will deliver him in time of trouble.

The Lord will preserve him, and keep him alive; and he shall be blessed upon the earth: and thou wilt not deliver him unto the will of his enemies. The Lord will strengthen him upon the bed of languishing: thou wilt make all his bed in his sickness." (Psalms 41:1-3 KJV)

There are seven strong promises to those who consider the poor listed here:

1. The Lord will deliver him in time of trouble.
2. The Lord will preserve him
3. and keep him alive
4. and he shall be blessed upon the earth:
5. and the Lord wilt not deliver him unto the will of his enemies.
6. The Lord will strengthen him upon the bed of languishing: (meaning that you will be strong in your old age)

And

7. He will make all his bed in his sickness.

Giving to the poor is directly related to your health and to every other area of your life! Amazingly there are very many

Muslims who practice giving to the poor. When they do this, they activate the law of God unknowingly and unlock blessings which God has prepared for anyone who does His will. What a wonderful God we serve!

"Whoso stoppeth his ears at the cry of the poor, he also shall cry himself, but shall not be heard." (Proverbs 21:13)

Many Christians prayers are not heard because of how they treat the poor! When you despise the poor, you actually despise God!

"He that oppresseth the poor reproacheth his Maker: but he that honoureth him hath mercy on the poor." (Proverbs 14:31 KJV)

"If I regard iniquity in my heart, the Lord will not hear me:" (Psalms 66:18)

To abandon the poor is considered iniquity by God!

"The rich man's wealth is his strong city: the destruction of the poor is their poverty."(Proverbs 10:15)

Poverty destroys mankind, it is a great enemy and no man should be forced to suffer this inhumane punishment. Nevertheless, many do. The vast majority of humanity languishes in poverty. This is a great injustice and God is not pleased with it. He will arise and plead their cause! That means He will punish the wicked for their injustice and this judgement will begin in the house of God before it proceeds out to the world!

> *"For the oppression of the poor, for the sighing of the needy, now will I arise, says the Lord:.." (Psalms 12:5)*

> *"Ye have shamed the council of the poor, because the Lord is his refuge." (Psalms 14:6)*

The Bible calls one who has mercy on the poor one who has a "bountiful eye." It simply means that you believe that if you give to them, there is plenty coming back to you and because you believe this thing, the Lord shall fulfill it.

> *"He that has a bountiful eye will be blessed for he gives of his bread to the poor."(Proverbs 22:9)*

> *"He that oppresseth the poor to increase his riches, and he that giveth to the rich, shall surely come to want." (Proverbs 22:16)*

We have already covered the fact that if you give to the rich instead of the poor, you will trigger the law of poverty and bring it upon your life. Satan knows this and he uses it against the church.

> *"Let him that stole steal no more: but rather let him labour, working with his hands the thing which is good, that he may have to give to him that needeth."(Ephesians 4:28 KJV)*

This one is in the New Testament just in case someone needs it repeated for the body of Christ. Jesus gave instructions in this area, but interestingly he gave no instructions concerning the tithe. I wonder why?

> *"Therefore when thou doest thine alms, do not sound a trumpet before thee, as the hypocrites do in the synagogues and in the streets, that they may have glory of men. Verily I say unto you, They have their reward. But when thou doest alms, let not thy left hand know what thy right hand doeth: That thine alms may be in secret: and thy Father which seeth in secret himself shall reward thee openly."(Matthew 6:2-4 KJV)*

Showing the world that you are giving to the poor is a quick way of forfeiting whatever blessing God had for you when you gave to the poor. Avoid hypocrisy, give in secret. Only reveal it to those who gave you their substance to give to the poor for accountability purposes. Otherwise you'll lose your blessing.

"There is that scattereth, and yet increaseth; and there is that withholdeth more than is meet, but it tendeth to poverty." (Proverbs 11:24)

An invisible law which causes the generous to increase and the selfish to become poorer and poorer. The greedy will end up poor, just wait and see.

"He that hath pity upon the poor lendeth unto the Lord; and that which he hath given will he pay him again." (Proverbs 19:17)

We have already explored how central banks make their fortunes through lending to banks which then promise to pay back those loans by collecting taxes from the citizenry. This makes you an unwitting slave and indeed, without Christ, you are a slave to your government which is a slave to the central bankers who are servants of Satan which means that without Christ, you ultimately are a slave to the devil. Whether you like it or not. The Luciferian central banks of this world lend to governments which enslave their citizens. But Christians can lend to God by taking pity on the poor and sharing their resources with them. God gives back everything we give Him with interest!

"Now unto him that is able to do exceeding abundantly above all that we ask or think, according

to the power that worketh in us" (Ephesians 3:20 KJV)

"No man can serve two masters: for either he will hate the one, and love the other;or else he will hold to the one, and despise the other. Ye cannot serve God and Mammon." (Matthew 6:24 KJV)

The only way to rebel against Satan and his economic system of slavery is to serve God. The way to flourish in the Kingdom of God is to do His will. The kingdom of darkness hoards greedily and selfishly for themselves. The Kingdom of God is the exact opposite. We give generously to the poor first and then we have far more to give to our churches, missions, and anywhere else where we can give.

"Jesus said unto him, If thou wilt be perfect, go and sell that thou hast, and give to the poor, and thou shalt have treasure in heaven: and come and follow me." Matthew 19:21 KJV

This is the financial system of the Kingdom of God. Do business and share what you make with the poor. This is how one reaches perfection in the Kingdom of God. God will cause your business to flourish. But once you are rich, don't forget. Life is not about earthly possessions, but living a holy life which is pleasing unto God and serving Him in Spirit and in truth.

"Charge them that are rich in this world, that they be not high minded, nor trust in uncertain riches, but in the living God, who gives us richly, all things to enjoy.

> *That they do good, that they be rich in good works, ready to distribute, willing to communicate. Laying up in store for themselves a good foundation against the time to come, that they may hold onto eternal life." (1 Timothy 6:17)*

Need more New Testament instructions to give to the poor? Ok!

> *"Only they would that we should remember the poor; the same which I also was forward to do." (Galatians 2:10)*

Please understand how frustrating it is when God commands us to do something and we refuse to simply obey.

"God standeth in the congregation of the mighty; he judgeth among the gods.

How long will ye judge unjustly, and accept the persons of the wicked? Selah.

Defend the poor and fatherless: do justice to the afflicted and needy Deliver the poor and needy: rid them out of the hand of the wicked. They know not, neither will they understand; they walk on in darkness: all the foundations of the earth are out of course. I have said, Ye are gods; and all of you are children of the most High. But ye shall die like men, and fall like one of the princes. Arise, O God, judge the earth: for thou shalt inherit all nations." (Psalms 82:1-8)

Now please follow these direct instructions: Psalms 82:3,4

Defend the poor and fatherless: do justice to the afflicted and needy.

Deliver the poor and needy: rid them out of the hand of the wicked."

When mankind refuses to obey God's commandments, He laments with the following words: Psalms 82:5-8

They know not, neither will they understand; they walk on in darkness: all the foundations of the earth are out of course.

I have said, Ye are gods; and all of you are children of the most High.

But ye shall die like men, and fall like one of the princes.

Arise, O God, judge the earth: for thou shalt inherit all nations."

Will you make the Lord sad? Or will you please His heart by obeying His commandments?

> *"He judged the cause of the poor and needy; then it was well with him: was not this to know me? saith the Lord." (Jeremiah 22:16 KJV)*

To know the Lord is to do justice to the poor and the needy. To share your resources with them and share the love of Christ with them. How is this not preached in churches all over the world?

> *"The Spirit of the Lord is upon me, because he hath anointed me to preach the gospel to the poor; he hath sent me to heal the brokenhearted, to preach deliverance to the captives, and recovering of sight to the blind, to set at liberty them that are bruised," (Luke 4:18)*

God's strategy to reach the poor with the gospel is brilliant because the poor are the vast majority of the people on the earth. According to the poverty world clock, there are almost one billion people living in extreme poverty. Even more live in average poverty. It is sad that the world bank supposedly has an agenda to end world poverty but the church has none. God has an agenda for this and it is through the church. But if the church is so busy tithing and rushing to the altar to give their seed after passing the homeless in the street and leaving them to starve, then God's plan is being interfered with. As a direct result of the COVID-19 man made pandemic, the world bank is expecting to see a rise in those plunged into poverty from 120 million additional people living in poverty as a result of the pandemic to 150 million by the end of 2021. According to the world bank, in 2018, four out of five people below the international poverty line lived in rural areas. -half of the poor are children. Women represent a majority of the poor in most regions and among some age groups.

Almost half of poor people in Sub-Saharan Africa live in just five countries:

Nigeria, the Democratic Republic of Congo, Tanzania, Ethiopia and Madagascar.

(Is this why we see no churches in the rural areas but far more churches in the cities where there are educated people with good jobs to pull tithes and offerings from?)

The above list is by no means exhaustive. Uganda, Rwanda, Burundi and many other countries worldwide have huge populations of poor people. Around 1.89 billion people or nearly 36% of the world's population live in extreme poverty. Nearly half the population in developing countries lives on less than $1.25 a day. - Worldvision

The truth is that the vast majority of the world's human population lives in poverty. But there is something which the church can do about this and in so doing, the body of Christ can win most of humanity to Christ if they will just do the right thing.

> *"If a brother or sister be naked, and destitute of daily food, And one of you say unto them, Depart in peace, be ye warmed and filled; notwithstanding ye give them not those things which are needful to the body; what doth it profit? Even so faith, if it hath not works, is dead, being alone." (James 2:15-17 KJV)*

Your Christian faith without works of charity is nothing but a form of godliness and denying the power thereof.

If you're in business, let your business be a machine which God uses to feed the hungry, shelter the homeless, clothe the naked and educate those who don't have school fees and you will see an explosive turn around.

> *"Learn to do well, seek judgement, relieve the oppressed, judge the fatherless, plead for the*

widow." (Isaiah 1:17)

"Open your mouth for the dumb in the cause of all such as are appointed to destruction. Open thy mouth, judge righteously and plead the cause of the poor and needy." (Proverbs 31:8,9)

"Rob not the poor, because he is poor: neither oppress the afflicted in the gate:For the Lord will plead their cause, and spoil the soul of those that spoiled them." (Proverbs 22:22,23)

"For ye have the poor always with you; but me ye have not always." (Matthew 26:11)

"Woe unto them that decree unrighteous decrees, and that write grievousness which they have prescribed; To turn aside the needy from judgment, and to take away the right from the poor of my people, that widows may be their prey, and that they may rob the fatherless! And what will ye do in the day of visitation, and in the desolation which shall come from far? to whom will ye flee for help? and where will ye leave your glory?" (Isaiah 10:1-3)

"But whoso hath this world's good, and seeth his brother have need, and shutteth up his bowels of compassion from him, how dwelleth the love of God

in him?" (1 John 3:17)

"And the word of the Lord came unto Zechariah, saying, Thus speaketh the Lord of hosts, saying, Execute true judgment, and shew mercy and compassions every man to his brother: And oppress not the widow, nor the fatherless, the stranger, nor the poor; and let none of you imagine evil against his brother in your heart." (Zachariah 7:8-10)

Jesus said,

"But when thou makest a feast, call the poor, the maimed, the lame, the blind:

And thou shalt be blessed; for they cannot recompense thee: for thou shalt be recompensed at the resurrection of the just." (Luke 14:13, 14)

"All things are lawful for me, but all things are not expedient: all things are lawful for me, but all things edify not. Let no man seek his own, but every man another's wealth." (1 Corinthians 10:23-24 KJV)

"He that despiseth his neighbour sinneth: but he that hath mercy on the poor, happy is he."(Proverbs 14:21 KJV)

"He hath dispersed, he hath given to the poor; his righteousness endureth for ever; his horn shall be exalted with honour. The wicked shall see it, and be grieved; he shall gnash with his teeth, and melt away: the desire of the wicked shall perish."(Psalms 112:9-10 KJV)

"He that oppresseth the poor reproacheth his Maker: but he that honoureth him hath mercy on the poor." (Proverbs 14:31 KJV)

The way that we honor God with our giving is mainly by giving to the poor.

"Wherefore the Lord God of Israel saith, I said indeed that thy house, and the house of thy father, should walk before me forever: but now the Lord saith, Be it far from me; for them that honour me I will honour, and they that despise me shall be lightly esteemed." (1 Samuel 2:30 KJV)

Jesus called those "spiritual leaders" who tithed, hypocrites, because they would not do justice or have mercy. Jesus considered justice, mercy and faith to be far more important matters of the law than tithing:

"Woe unto you, scribes and Pharisees, hypocrites! for ye pay tithe of mint and anise and cummin,

and have omitted the weightier matters of the law, judgment, mercy, and faith: these ought ye to have done, and not to leave the other undone." (Matthew 23:23 KJV)

Please don't be offended if you are a tither. Jesus is simply showing you a better way to give to Him. If the tithe belongs to the Lord, then we can see how to give to the Lord directly, by giving to the poor.

God will honor those that honor Him!

Those that do not shall be cast away. God separates those that give to the poor and those who do not in Matthew 25.

"When the Son of man shall come in his glory, and all the holy angels with him, then shall he sit upon the throne of his glory: And before him shall be gathered all nations: and he shall separate them one from another, as a shepherd divideth his sheep from the goats: And he shall set the sheep on his right hand, but the goats on the left. Then shall the King say unto them on his right hand, Come, ye blessed of my Father, inherit the kingdom prepared for you from the foundation of the world:

For I was an hungred, and ye gave me meat: I was thirsty, and ye gave me drink:

I was a stranger, and ye took me in: Naked, and ye clothed me: I was sick, and ye visited me: I was in prison, and ye came unto me. Then shall the righteous answer him, saying, Lord, when saw we thee an hungred, and fed thee? or thirsty, and gave thee drink? When saw we thee a stranger, and took thee in? or naked, and clothed thee? Or when saw we thee sick, or in prison, and came unto thee? And the King shall answer and say unto them, Verily I say unto you, Inasmuch as ye have done it unto one of the least of these my brethren, ye have done it unto me. Then shall he say also unto them on the left hand, Depart from me, ye cursed, into everlasting fire, prepared for the devil and his angels: For I was an hungred, and ye gave me no meat: I was thirsty, and ye gave me no drink: I was a stranger, and ye took me not in: naked, and ye clothed me not: sick, and in prison, and ye visited me not.

Then shall they also answer him, saying, Lord, when saw we thee an hungred, or athirst, or a stranger, or naked, or sick, or in prison, and did not minister unto thee?

> *Then shall he answer them, saying, Verily I say unto you, Inasmuch as ye did it not to one of the least of these, ye did it not to me. And these shall go away into everlasting punishment: but the righteous into life eternal." (Matthew 25:31-46 KJV)*

This is why my wife and I formed the Worldshare Foundation to give food, clothing, shelter and medical care to those in extreme poverty in Uganda and the rest of East Africa. Please feel free to check out our website:

www.lifeisspiritual.org

Find out how you can give to those in dire need and be the very hands of the Lord to meet them at their point of need. May God richly bless you and favor you in Jesus' precious holy name!

CHAPTER EIGHT

A Roadmap to Raising Capital

The primary purpose of Christian financial education is to empower parents to work towards making passive income. When parents earn passive income, they have more time to pay attention to raising their families in the fear of God. If both parents are away from home, working at a job, the children are left at home being taught evil and witchcraft by cartoons on television. Furthermore, when parents earn passive income, they're able to enjoy financial freedom and pass those benefits down to their children as well.

There are three types of income.

- Earned Income (This is salary income or a paycheck given to someone in exchange for their time and service). This form of income is for employees and is taxed the highest of all forms of income. Furthermore, the employee is taxed AGAIN while making purchases in the form of value added tax (VAT) so in the end the employee is taxed coming and going. This is very unfortunate.
- Portfolio Income. This income includes but is not limited

to stock shares in companies, bonds, equity traded funds (ETFs) etc... These are also called paper assets.

- Passive Income. This is income which keeps coming into your pocket whether you are present to supervise it or not. An example of this is rents paid by your tenants who live in your property and pay you rent every month.

Earned income is money you work for. Portfolio and passive income is money that works for you. The key to becoming wealthy is the ability to convert earned income into passive income and/or portfolio income as quickly as possible.

The least taxed income is passive income. The government taxes the income you work hard for (in employment) rather than the income your money works hard to make you rich. The problem with our education system is that it only trains students to be highly educated employees. Although there are some institutions where entrepreneurship is taught, an in-depth teaching on money, it's history and the past, present and future of capitalism, is still missing from the curriculums. So graduates are sent out into the world to only look for jobs and if they don't get jobs, they join the country's unemployed and find themselves going back to be a financial burden on their society (through crime) or on their parents, who have already sold all of their possessions in order to pay school fees. These fees they paid do not guarantee job placements and therefore, a return on their investment may be out of the question.

According to the Kenya National Bureau of Statistics 2015/2016 Labor Force basic report, Kenya's unemployment rate was at 7.4%. So basically there were about 2,960,000 jobless Kenyans out of a population of 40,000,000 in 2016. The rate of unemployment is even higher in our neighboring countries of Uganda and Tanzania. Thankfully this financial education works for anyone in any civilized country. The unemployment rate of 7.4% is far lower than the actual number today but the information tells us something very important.

Financial illiteracy (financial ignorance) leads to the creation of wage slaves. A wage-slave based economy is the worst kind of economy a nation can possibly have. The truth is that if you choose financial security (employment) instead of financial freedom (financial intelligence, investment and entrepreneurship), in the end, you will end up with neither. Unfortunately, the university is a great place to train people to have cash flow out of their pockets and into the pockets of the rich. Students graduate heavily in debt, then they get into the job market to find a good job, then they get into more debt and watch their cash flow to the government through income taxes. The more they earn, the higher the percentage they pay in taxes. The harder you work in a job the more you make and the more taxes you pay. It's almost like the government penalizes you for working harder. Those who seek financial freedom must gain the skills of a capitalist. Develop skills in the business and investment departments. Develop the proper mental and emotional attitudes towards your investment decisions. An intelligent investor is defined as one who is patient, intelligent and eager to learn. You must also be able to harness your emotions and think for yourself.

Being an intelligent investor is more a matter of character, than brain. An investment operation is one which, upon thorough analysis, promises safety of principle (capital) and an adequate or infinite return on investment. People who invest make money for themselves, people who work jobs make money for their employers. Money only accentuates the money pattern flowing through your head. In other words, your money is only doing what you have commanded it to do through your own thoughts, words and actions. The truth is that corporations buy employees wholesale and sell them retail on the open market. The employers hire employees because whatever the employer is paying the employee is far less than what the employer makes from the employee's labor. If it were not so, the employer would soon go out of business. I do not condemn this system. I simply advocate for awareness of the nature of the system so as to foster a mentality of growth and development in our people for a brighter future.

There is something called financial aptitude, it is what you do with money once you have it, how you protect it from being taken from you, how you are able to keep it longer and how you make that money work for you.

People struggle financially because they do not understand financial aptitude and the nature of cash flow. A person can be very academically and professionally successful and still be financially illiterate. Having a lack of investment capital (paying debts and bills instead of purchasing assets) results in one missing out on the "investment experience." Most are never able to become what the investment world calls "sophisticated investors." The best investments are usually sold to sophisticated investors, who then turn around and sell them to the people who are "playing it safe." You see the average person is never prepared for the deal of a lifetime when it presents itself. As a result, their financial fortunes never change. Wealth can be defined as a person's ability to survive so many days forward or, if I stopped working today, how long could I survive?

There are three basic ways of raising the capital and you will need to obtain an asset which gives you passive income.

- From Investors - Venture Capitalists are always looking for someone they can trust with their money to bring back a good return on their investment.

- From Your Customers - The customers you sell goods and services to are a major way to obtain the capital you need to start your passive income business.

- From your job -This way of acquiring capital for a passive income investment requires that you adjust what you do with your salary when you get it. If one will follow the rules I've written for you below, you will raise the capital you need for your first investment.

So how can you begin to move from financial slavery to financial freedom? Follow these steps!

1. **Rule Number One: Thou Shalt Pay Thyself**

"There is treasure to be desired and oil in the dwelling of the wise; but a foolish man spendeth it up." (Proverbs 21:20)

Every time you get paid, whether it is a salary, a bonus, a grant, a Christmas present, whatever the case may be. Take 10% or 20% or more and put it aside into savings every time money passes through your hands. This percentage of your money may seem small, but over time it builds up through compound interest. Albert Einstein called compound interest the most powerful force in the world. He called it the 8th wonder of the world, "he who understands it, earns it, he who does not, pays it." Paying yourself a percentage every time you get paid is compounding your savings which causes it to grow exponentially.

A presidential candidate puts his vote into his own ballot box during the election. That is exactly what you should do every time you get paid. Failing to pay oneself every time you get paid is a financial sin. Every time you pay yourself, you're making an investment into your future. It is a small financial seed you sow into yourself. Then every time you pay yourself, you are watering that plant, and every time you water it, it grows a little bit.

If you pay yourself first, you get financially stronger, mentally and financially. If you pay yourself last, you get weaker in both ways. This is an area of financial self-discipline. Those who lack self-discipline will become victims of those who have it. Becoming wealthy in a Godly way has everything to do with self-improvement, self-determination and personal character building. Failing to pay yourself a little bit every time you get paid is basically investing into the future of everyone else except yourself. This is bad financial behavior and a financial sin. If you keep setting aside 10%, one day you will have enough to take the next step.

One of the worst financial habits you can possibly have is dipping into savings to pay bills. The rich know that savings are only used to create more money, not to pay bills. People go to school so that they can learn a profession and work for money, but it is more important to learn how to make money work for you. Again, if money is smarter than you, you will work for it all your life, but if you are smarter than it, then it will serve you well. In order to be the master of money, you need to be smarter than it, then money will do as it is told.

2. Rule Number Two: Invest in Cash Flow assets, Not cash flow liabilities!

"Where no oxen are, the manger is clean, but much revenue comes by the strength of the ox." (Proverbs 14:4 NIV)

After your savings grow, you will one day find yourself ready to invest. When you're ready, invest in cash flow assets, not liabilities. An asset, as far as this book is concerned, is simply any investment that puts money into your pocket regularly, whether you are there to supervise it or not. It is an "ox" as far as proverbs 14:4 is concerned. It brings much revenue.

An example of an "Ox" could be a bus. Every day it can bring you cash $ by carrying passengers from point A to point

B. That is passive income since you will hire the driver and the staff to work for you. Their salaries come from the income the bus makes. You get paid every day. One should have plenty of oxen.

Conversely, a liability is anything that takes money out of your pocket. This includes rent, school fees, electricity, food, water, gas, phone bill, the house you live in, your personal vehicle etc. Everyone has liabilities, but not everyone has assets. The key here is to invest in cash flow assets which keep paying you. One should focus his efforts into working hard to acquire cash flow assets.

Most broke people are liability rich and asset poor. Everyone has been in a situation where they overheard someone selling a very expensive item for a throw away price because they needed the money right away. At that moment was your opportunity to buy an expensive asset for very little money. If you did not have the money, then opportunity came your way, but you missed it. After such events, one learns the lesson: One must take advantage of the opportunity of a lifetime, during the lifetime of the opportunity.

> *"I returned and saw under the sun, that the race is not to the swift, nor the battle to the strong, neither yet bread to the wise, nor yet riches to men of*

understanding, nor yet favor to men of skill; but time and chance happen to them all." (Ecclesiastes 9:11)

Preparing for opportunities puts you in a better position to be ready when the opportunity presents itself. Make sure the opportunity is legitimate, there's an old saying that goes, "when the deal is too good, think twice."

Another one says, "a fool and his gold are quickly parted." Investment calls for discernment, if you mess up, don't be afraid to try again. This time, you will have the added advantage of experience on your side. The rewards of success are well worth it.

The following two charts demonstrate the different money mindsets of a rich man and a poor man.

The rich man has cash flow assets which pay for his liabilities (expenses). The poor man relies on his job salary to cover all his expenses and then wonders why he's broke at the end of the month.

The Rich Man's Mindset

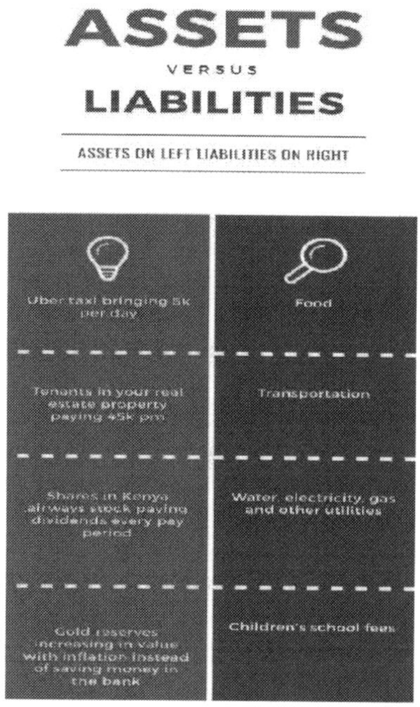

The rich man's mindset towards his money is based on financial intelligence. He understands that his cash flow assets should pay for his liabilities. He focuses on building his assets and avoids purchasing more liabilities than he absolutely must have. Every time he wants to purchase a liability, e.g. big flat screen television, personal car, etc. he first adds a cash flow asset to his asset column, then he buys the liability. This is financial intelligence asset management. The house you live in is not an asset if it does not put money into your pocket every day. Even if it increases in value over time, it does not send cash flow into your pocket. During the 2008 housing crisis in the U.S. many people thought their homes were assets until the market crashed, then they found out that their homes were liabilities and many people lost their homes altogether. The rich man understands the difference between assets and liabilities.

Wealth is the measure of the cash flow from the asset column compared to the expense column. Wealth is equal to more assets than liabilities. Wealth is increasing assets and decreasing liabilities. The rich buy cash flow assets, the poor only have liabilities and expenses, the middle class buy liabilities they think are assets so they can show off to "friends" who are also broke!

Professional skills allow the "university educated" to enter into the workforce and work for money, which essentially means that they work for:

1. The company's owners
2. The government (through taxes)
3. 3)The bank (through debts)

But rarely, if ever, do they work for themselves. The rich mind their own business, the poor mind the business of others, usually the rich. If you work for money, you give the power to your employer. If money works for you, you keep the power and control it. Every dollar invested in assets becomes a great employee, working hard to create more employees. This means you're getting richer.

One of the things that hold us back is some degree of self-doubt. Thc lack of sclf-confidcncc, onc may cvcn know what to do, but lack the courage to act on it. Oftentimes, in the real world, it is not the smart that get ahead, but the bold. In 1 Samuel 17 we read about the story of how Israel went out to fight against the Philistines and their giant, Goliath, who defied the God of Israel. The "smart" soldiers refused to fight against Goliath who had called to the entire army of Israel for one soldier who could defeat him. For days, the standoff continued. Finally, David heard about the words of Goliath and with pure boldness, beat Goliath with a stone and a sling and went on to become the king's son in law, passing all of the "smart" Hebrew soldiers. David went on to become king of Israel. Victory and dominion belong to the bold.

The poor man on the other hand has a long list of cash flow liabilities and a short list of cash flow assets or even no assets at all. This keeps the poor man poor because every time he gets money, he keeps making poor decisions.

"The Poor Man's Mindset"

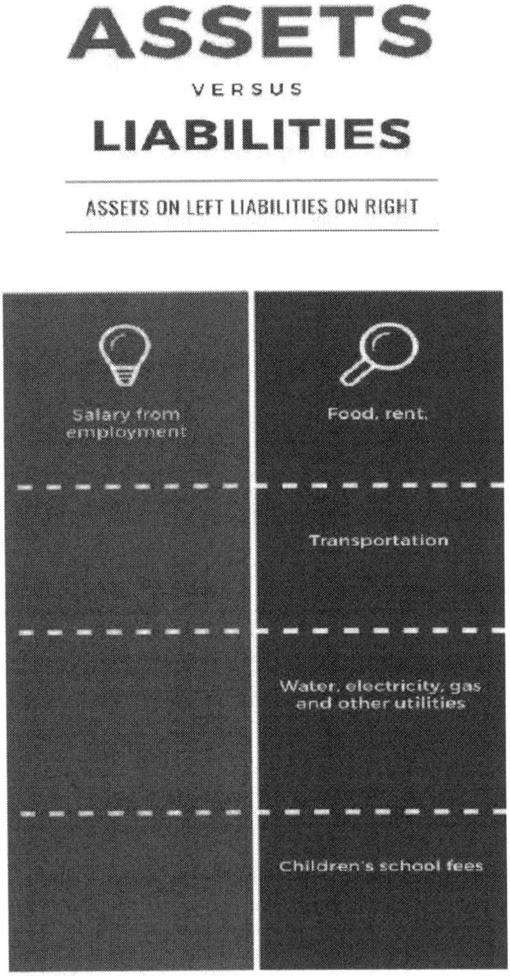

The poor man shows a lack of financial intelligence. He has one source of income and no assets to pay for his liabilities. Yet this model of financial behavior is what most university students that graduate from school are looking for. Without financial intelligence, they emerge as university graduates into a capitalist world poorly prepared for a ruthless and unforgiving financial system designed to enrich the financially intelligent and punish the financially ignorant, Christians included. The poor man gets an opportunity to purchase a personal vehicle and jumps at the chance, not knowing that a vehicle is not an asset, it is a liability. Value added tax, insurance, maintenance, gas and spare parts are now eating out of his pockets. He bought the car to impress people and show the world "he's arrived," and in so doing fell for the trap that many poor people fall into. The poverty trap of "instant gratification." Indeed, pride comes before destruction.

> *"Pride goes before destruction, and a haughty spirit before stumbling." (Proverbs 16:18)*

It is impossible to be rich, while continually making poor financial decisions. Whether you're saved or not. He should have invested his money in a high performance cash flow asset, not a personal car (which is a liability).

Making the decision to become financially intelligent is one of the decisions that separates the rich from the poor. These principles apply to all, whether they are Christians or not. One of the keys of wealth creation is delayed gratification. I have written this book to benefit Christians because I know true Christians will distribute the resources they get from the wealth they accrue to ease the suffering in the world and to build the Kingdom of God.

Remember what Jesus said:

> *"He that is faithful in that which is least is faithful also in much: and he that is unjust in the least is unjust also in much." (Luke 16:10)*

If you can be self-disciplined to pay yourself 10% every time you get paid and never spend it until you get an opportunity to invest in a high performance cash flow asset, then the scripture applies to you, if you're faithful with little things, you'll be faithful with big ones. This is money management. Anything you fail to manage, you will lose.

3. Knowledge is the real money.

Wealthy people decided to focus on cash flow consistently. Building apartments and renting out the space for cash flow is some of what the rich do. In the world of money, the rich are sellers and the poor and middle class are the buyers. One of the skills I learned from my dad, Pastor Victor Mwangi, is the skill of selling. He became a very skillful salesman in the U.S. Many of the skills he acquired he passed on to me. Then he sent me out into the world to sell water purifiers to sink or swim! I learned how to swim quick! You must focus on selling and not on buying. So many people are cash poor because they love to buy and hate to sell! Sell more than you buy and a whole new world of possibilities will open up for you. To sell, one must develop their personal self-confidence and be very optimistic. God works with optimism.

In 2 Kings 7, we read about four leprous men who were outside the city walls during the time that the Syrians had besieged Samaria. The optimism of these four lepers gave God an opportunity to liberate the children of Israel.

> *'Then Elisha said, 'Listen to the word of the LORD; thus says the LORD, 'Tomorrow about this time a measure of fine flour will be sold for a shekel, and two measures of barley for a shekel, in the gate of Samaria.' The royal officer on whose hand the king was leaning answered the man of God and said, "Behold, if the LORD should make windows in heaven, could this thing be?" Then he said, "Behold, you will see it with your own eyes, but you will not eat of it." (2 Kings 7:1-2)*

Four lepers caused the Syrians to flee!

> *"Now there were four leprous men at the entrance of the gate; and they said to one another, "Why do we sit here until we die? "If we say, 'We will enter the city,' then the famine is in the city and we will die there; and if we sit here, we die also. Now therefore*

come, and let us go over to the camp of the Syrians. If they spare us, we will live; and if they kill us, we will but die." They arose at twilight to go to the camp of the Arameans; when they came to the outskirts of the camp of the Syrians, behold, there was no one there. For the Lord had caused the army of the Syrians to hear a sound of chariots and a sound of horses, even the sound of a great army, so that they said to one another, "Behold, the king of Israel has hired against us the kings of the Hittites and the kings of the Egyptians, to come upon us." Therefore they arose and fled in the twilight, and left their tents and their horses and their donkeys, even the camp just as it was, and fled for their life. When these lepers came to the outskirts of the camp, they entered one tent and ate and drank, and carried from there silver and gold and clothes, and went and hid them; and they returned and entered another tent and carried from there also, and went and hid them. Then they said to one another, "We are not doing right. This day is a day of good news, but we are keeping silent; if we wait until morning light, punishment will overtake us. Now therefore come, let us go and tell the king's household." So they came and called to the gatekeepers of the city, and they told them, saying, "We came to the camp of the Syrians, and behold, there was no one there, nor the voice of man, only the horses tied and the donkeys tied, and the tents just as they were."The gatekeepers called and told it within the king's household. Then the king arose in the night and said to his servants, "I will now tell you what the Syrians have done to us. They know that we are hungry; therefore, they have gone from the camp to hide themselves in the field, saying, 'When they come out of the city, we will capture them alive and get into the city." One of his servants said, "Please, let some men take five of the horses which remain, which are left in the city. Behold, they will be in any case like all the multitude of Israel who are left in it; behold, they will be in any case like all the multitude of Israel who have already perished, so let us send and see." They took therefore two chariots with horses, and the king sent after the army of the Aramean's, saying, "Go and see." They went after them to the Jordan, and behold, all the way was full of clothes and equipment which the Aramean's had thrown away in their haste. Then the messengers returned and told the king. So the people went out and plundered the camp of the Syrians. Then a measure of fine flour was sold for a shekel and two measures of barley for a shekel, according to the word of the LORD. (2 Kings 7:1-16)

In 2 Kings 6:24 we read that Ben Hadad, king of Syria had gathered his army and went up and besieged Samaria. The famine was so great that the price of everyday food commodities had skyrocketed. A donkey's head was now four score pieces of silver (80 pieces of silver) and the forth part of a cab of dove's dung was five pieces of silver. You can imagine how bad things must have been if a portion of dove droppings cost 5 pieces of silver! But by the time the word of Elisha the prophet of God had been fulfilled, the price of commodities like a measure of fine flour had come back down to just a shekel and two measures of barley had come down to ashekel. All this price variation in the marketplace had taken place because of the word of the Lord and four optimistic lepers. Let what you sell be a derivative of your life's mission statement. We spoke about derivatives in the previous chapters. Wine is a derivative of grapes. Let what you're selling be a derivative of your life story or mission statement.

4. **Learn the rules of taxes, debt, inflation and retirement.**

These forces can help to make you rich, or they can help to make you poor. The average employee has taxes, debt, inflation and savings for a retirement plan taken out of their paycheck before they get paid. In other words, everyone gets paid before you! Most of an employee's money is spent to cover living expenses like taxes, debt, inflation and savings for a retirement plan and thus goes into the pockets of the conspirators. This is why there is no financial education in schools.

The stock market is risky, the average person has little control over the stock market and the odds are that the market will crash and take most of their money with it. Better to put your retirement money into your own pocket, not the pockets of those who control the NSSF or the NHIF or Wall Street for that matter. With a financial education, one does not need to pay a security fund to lose their money. We saw how both the NSSF and the NHIF were involved in scandals where billions in hard earned taxpayer monies have disappeared. The U.S. is no different, the 2008 housing market crash proved that. Subprime mortgage derivatives were given a AAA credit score by rating agencies such as Standard & Poor's, a financial services company, a division of S&P Global. S&P publishes financial research on stocks, bonds and commodities. Now that these financial vehicles(derivatives) proved to be far below AAA, who will rate the ratings agencies that gave a green light to rotten financial products resulting in a global recession? Once bitten, twice shy.

The rich use taxes, debt, inflation and retirement savings to their advantage. Focus on investments, increase business and personal assets to earn more money. (IGAs-Income Generating Assets) By simply changing one's focus, you can change your financial outcome. Focus on increasing your assets. This will in turn increase your income. By focusing on increasing assets, you pay less in taxes, then use debt to acquire more assets and watch as inflation increases your cash flow which means rather than sending retirement savings to NSSF, or wasting money on premiums to NHIF you can pay for a high quality health insurance policy from a reputable, international insurance company and you can put your money in your pocket via cash flow from businesses and personal assets. That's smart money. Even in your retirement you will not need to rely on NSSF (where your money may or may not disappear in the next scandal), your assets will provide more than enough tax free (or at least taxed far less than retirement funds) cash flow to sustain you and your children.

Every month cash flows to NSSF/NHIF, to invest in funds to bankroll managers in the form of commissions, salaries, bonuses, housing allowances, transportation allowances, and fees. Then when member tax payers are old and feeble, their retirement cash is sent upcountry in the form of pension/ retirement checks (cheques). Then after they die, this cash is taxed again as it flows into the funeral home and to the government in the form of taxes for what they left behind.

Here is the "rule of thumb"! The harder employees work, the more cash flows to the rich. Schools do not teach students about cash flow, students are simply advised to do well in school so that they can go to the university and graduate top of their class and then get a job, which is just training to give their cash back to the rich and work hard to make the rich even richer. With the amount of money, they paid in school fees, they could have invested in a cash flow asset which would have doubled itself and paid off its initial investment by graduation time. Then they could have used the passive income to pay university tuition if they still wanted to, and still have steady income during their school years and after they graduate whether they get a job or not! Even a motorbike (Boda Boda) with a hired driver who must bring Kshs 1,000 per day will net the student Kshs 30,000 per month passive income. Meanwhile the university cannot even guarantee the student a job after graduation even if he passes with top honors! We read about one university graduate who was offered Kshs 10,000 ($100) a month salary!

Without financial education, we are doomed to repeat the financial mistakes of the previous generation. One should never forget, everything in this world belongs to God. We are simply stewards of His resources. He has entrusted them to us. What we do with it shows whether we are faithful managers or not.

> *"The silver is Mine and the gold is Mine,' declares the LORD of hosts. (Haggai 2:1)*

It is possible to print your own money. I know you may be shocked, but I do not mean counterfeiting money.

The way you print your own money is through a financial principle known as ROI (Return On Investment).

Most bankers, or real estate brokers, will tell you that a 5% to 12% ROI is a good return on your money. But those are returns for someone without much financial intelligence. It is possible to make infinite returns on your investments. The way you print your money is by receiving an infinite return on your money. The definition I use for an infinite return is "continuous cash flow." Basically, you print your own money when you get back all the money you invested in a cash flow asset, plus you still own the asset and enjoy the benefits of the cash flow from the asset. Financial intelligence at its best. With strong financial intelligence, you can print your own money via a business, real estate (which I encourage everyone to gain knowledge about), stocks, and even commodities such as gold, silver & oil. Again, the key is going for an infinite return, getting money continuously for being wise.

Certain words program the minds of people and condition/teach/program them to steal from themselves and further enrich those who are already wealthy. I believe that the prince of the power of the air has bewitched masses of everyday people to think in self-defeating ways (Christians included) and rob themselves with the following spells which are told to us by people who are older than us as we are growing up.

Here is an example of what we are told in order to program our minds for slavery:

- Taxes: "Go to school to get a job. These words program a child to become an employee who pays the highest percentage of their income in taxes. By getting a job, you are exchanging your time for money. You are working for money, instead of money working for you. When you realize who you are in Christ, you begin to fulfill your purpose, and when you do so, you are able to earn an income without being enslaved by using wisdom. Instead, you're paid for doing what God has called you to do. That is part of becoming a master over money, instead of money being a master over you. If you do not learn to outsmart money, then money (or the lack thereof) will rule over you until you leave this world. This book outlines how to view money through the eyes of financial wisdom.

- Debt: "Buy a house. Your house is an asset and your biggest investment." This is one of the biggest lies of the devil because this is preparation for bad debt. Often your house is ***not*** your biggest asset, it's your biggest liability. It does not put money in your pocket IF you are the one living in it. The only way you can be making money is if you sublet your home and generate cash flow from your tenant or move out completely and rent out the whole place for rent cash flow. There is good debt and bad debt. Let's start with the bad. Bad debt is the kind of debt you find yourself in after buying a liability. Like going into debt to buy a personal vehicle which is also costing you money to maintain. Bad debt is any debt which does not help you obtain cash flow assets. Good debt is the kind of debt which for example allows you to build an apartment complex using the bank's money (TBM), then use the monthly cash flow from the tenants to pay down the debt you owe the bank until you no longer owe them, but you still own the apartment and so now you have a license to print money and keep cash flowing into your pocket whether you are present or not.

- Inflation: What they tell you: "Save Your Money." When you save money in a bank, you unwittingly increase inflation, which actually devalues your savings. Due to the fractional reserve system of banking. The bank can take your money and lend it out several times, charging much more interest on the loans than the saver receives for his/her savings. In other words, savers cause their own erosion of their purchasing power. The more they save, the more inflation increases. For every dollar you save, you give the bank license to print more money. It's better to keep your money moving, invest it into more cash flow assets so that inflation only increases the amount of money flowing your way.

- Retirement: "Invest for the long term in the National Social Security Fund (NSSF - Kenya's version of Wall Street's 401k or Roth IRAs) so that when you retire, they pay you monthly for your upkeep in retirement." This programming makes the managing directors in NSSF very rich for the long term. Why should you give your savings and retirement money to people in NSSF when you can have a license to print money by using financial knowledge and intelligence?

As we covered in previous chapters, NSSF is involved in financial scandals where billions of taxpayer's money has disappeared. Why should you flush your hard earned money down the toilet? Take charge of your own financial future.

NSSF may disappoint you during your retirement years. Billions in taxpayer monies have disappeared and nobody has been sent to prison. Are you willing to risk your finances for retirement in the hands of those who cannot give an account for their actions?

People are hungry for relevant financial education that is simply explained and easy to understand.

Many people are scared, frustrated and let down by our politicians and the economy. This is not just in Africa; in the U.S. the same thing is happening. Financial education will help you take your financial future into your own hands and will enable you to leave an inheritance for your children and your children's children.

5. Start Your Own Corporation

In life you will have two financial options. Either you will:

A. Work hard as an employee, pay 50% taxes. Save what is left, make your boss richer and retire

Or

B. Take the time to develop your financial intelligence. Add to the asset column and then form a corporation so that your money can be protected from paying high taxes like employees. A corporation does not pay taxes until it makes a profit. This can take years. A corporation can take its profits and reinvest in the corporation in order to expand and then whatever is left of the profits, pay a percentage in taxes.

Part of building your financial education is developing these four main technical skills.

- Accounting. This is financial literacy or the ability to read numbers.
- Investing. This is the science of money making money.
- Understanding markets.Understanding markets is the science of supply and demand. Sell what people are buying. Find out what people need, then supply it. This is valuable research on your part. Multinational companies pay their research departments very well. Can you see why?
- The Law. The law area is becoming aware of accounting, state and corporate regulations. A lawyer can help you protect your money. Rich people do not keep anything in their names, they keep it in their company name. This way if you are sued, and you lose the case, your wealth is protected, since you are a separate legal entity from your corporation.

The more sophisticated you get, the more opportunities will come your way. It is not gambling if you know what you're doing. It is gambling if you're just throwing money into a deal and praying. Invest more in your financial education than anything else.

> *"An hypocrite with his mouth destroyeth his neighbor: but through knowledge shall the just be delivered." (Proverbs 11:9)*

Great opportunities will not be seen with your eyes. They are seen with your mind. The brighter your mind, the further you can see. Books are filled with light. The more you learn, the brighter you become.

> *"And such as do wickedly against the covenant shall he corrupt by flatteries: but the people that do know their God shall be strong, and do exploits." (Daniel 11:32)*

> *"Give instruction to a wise man, and he will be yet wiser: teach a just man and he will increase in learning." (Proverbs 9:9)*

Remain consistent in learning.

> *"The hand of the diligent shall bear rule: but the slothful shall be under tribute." (Proverbs 12:24)*

Even those in full time ministry should also have investments in their minds first, and then also in assets. Especially if your ministry does not make enough money to support you and your family. I have heard ministers saying that "God told me to stop doing business and start doing full time ministry," even when the ministry is still in its infant stages bringing much financial struggle and suffering on the family. As a result, children can grow to resent the church because of hardship and scarcity of resources. This is not good. But God's word can never change.

> *"In the morning sow thy seed, and in the evening withhold not thine hand: for thou knowest not whether shall prosper, either this or that, or whether they both shall be alike good." (Ecclesiastes 11:6)*

It is possible to do both. Do business and ministry. If the ministry is in its baby stages, you will not need to give it 100% of your time. Doing business and ministry is actually encouraged in the Bible.

The wisdom of God's word can help save you a lot of heartache and pain. Even if you're not in ministry, you may have a job somewhere. Don't just quit suddenly. When you come home from work, don't rest, go into your other business and work hard on it. God's word says you do not know which of them will prosper, either this one or that one, or maybe both will alike do well.

God's word is filled with principles of investment.

"Cast your bread on the surface of the waters, for you will find it after many days.

Divide your portion to seven, or even to eight, for you do not know what misfortune may occur on the earth." (Ecclesiastes 11:1,2 NASB)

Casting your bread upon the waters refers to investment. We have already covered the similarities between water and finances. Dividing your portion to seven and even to eight simply means diversifying your investment portfolio. This will give you seven or more streams of income. If the bible suggests that you have many streams of income, imagine how financially stable our Heavenly Father wants us to be?

> *"Let them shout for joy, and be glad, that favor my righteous cause: yea, let them say continually, Let the LORD be magnified, which hath pleasure in the prosperity of his servant." (Psalms 35:27)*

Poverty is an enemy.

> *"The Lord shall cause thine enemies that rise up against thee to be smitten before thy face: they shall come out against thee one way, and flee before thee*

seven ways." (Deuteronomy 28:7)

If poverty is fleeing before you seven ways, that is seven revenue streams of income.

"And he shall be like a tree planted by the rivers of water, that brings forth his fruit in his season; his leaf also shall not whither; and whatsoever he doeth shall prosper." (Psalms 1:3)

Being planted by the rivers of water is being planted on top of the river-bank. The bank guides the flow of currency (money). You will be planted on top of the bank, instead of the bank being planted on top of you. "Your leaf also shall not whither," means your legal paperwork and documents shall be in order and keep increasing and will not fade away and whatsoever you do will succeed. That is God's amazing promise to you. No gimmicks, no strings attached, no sowing for financial miracles, just straight financial intelligence and wisdom.

The main reason any Christian should want wealth is to feed the hungry, clothe the naked, shelter the homeless and teach God's word to those who they help. The purpose of Christian wealth is the building of the Kingdom of God.

"Lay not up for yourselves treasures upon earth, where moth and rust doth corrupt, and where thieves

> *break through and steal: But lay up for yourselves treasures in heaven, where neither moth nor rust doth corrupt, and where thieves do not break through nor steal: For where your treasure is, there will your heart be also." (Matthew 16:19-21)*

Every time you use your resources to help others in acts of kindness, you lay up treasures in heaven.

> *"And the King shall answer and say unto them, Verily I say unto you, inasmuch as ye have done it unto one of the least of these my brethren, ye have done it unto me." (Matthew 25:40)*

Every day, with every penny you touch, you decide whether you will be rich, or poor. Many are afraid to invest because the pain of losing money is greater than the joy of being rich. They need FOCUS.

FOCUS Simply means Follow One Course Until Successful. Only an arrogant person would reject such financial information. The problem with arrogance is that it causes one to believe that what they do not know, does not matter. Remember, every day, with every amount of money you touch, you decide whether you will be rich, middle class or poor.

Finally, the three pillars of wealth are:

Stock and Bond Investing (that is the buying and selling of shares in company stock)

Real Estate (This involves but is not limited to construction, buying of land, property development and either selling the same for capital gains or renting the property out for cash flow).

Entrepreneurship (This involves starting your own business, learning what works and what does not and growing with your business until successful).

One fact remains whether you are saved or not. You must gain control over money, or the lack of it will always confine you to a very small circle. The extent of your financial activities will often be limited by the circumference of your knowledge.

CHAPTER NINE

God The Investor

Remember that God has made a significant investment in you. Just keeping you alive every day is an investment on God's part. He sends His angels to watch over you.

"For He shall give His angels charge over you, to keep you in all your ways.

> *In their hands they shall bear you up, Lest you dash your foot against a stone." (Psalms 91:11-12*

These angels must also eat.

> *"Man did eat angels' food: he sent them meat to the full." (Psalms 78:25)*

If God is feeding the angels He sends to preserve us, can you imagine the investment He is making into your life if the angels have been watching over you since your childhood? (Conversely, if the fallen angels must also eat, can you imagine what they are eating? Does God feed them? No! Because a Kingdom divided against itself will fall! Then what do they eat? They eat humanity.

"Be sober, be vigilant; because your adversary the devil, as a roaring lion, walketh about, seeking whom he may devour:" (1 Peter 5:8)

So the urgency of the gospel becomes even more obvious!) But back to our topic,

"Take heed that ye despise not one of these little ones; for I say unto you, that in heaven their angels do always behold the face of my Father which is in heaven." - Jesus Christ (Matthew 18:10)

This should tell you that our Heavenly Father is an investor. A very loving investor. He is also very wise, so He expects a return on His investment.

"For the kingdom of heaven is as a man travelling into a far country, who called his own servants, and delivered unto them his goods. And unto one he gave five talents, to another two, and to another one; to every man according to his several ability; and straightway took his journey. Then he that had received the five talents went and traded with the same, and made them other five talents. And likewise he that had received two, he also gained other two. But he that had received one went and digged in the earth, and hid his lord's money. After a long time

the lord of those servants cometh, and reckoneth with them. And so he that had received five talents came and brought other five talents, saying, Lord, thou deliveredst unto me five talents: behold, I have gained beside them five talents more. His lord said unto him, well done, thou good and faithful servant: thou hast been faithful over a few things, I will make thee ruler over many things: enter thou into the joy of thy lord. He also that had received two talents came and said, Lord, thou deliveredst unto me two talents: behold, I have gained two other talents beside them. His lord said unto him, well done, good and faithful servant; thou hast been faithful over a few things, I will make thee ruler over many things: enter thou into the joy of thy lord. Then he which had received the one talent came and said, Lord, I knew thee that thou art an hard man, reaping where thou hast not sown, and gathering where thou hast not strawed: And I was afraid, and went and hid thy talent in the earth: lo, there thou hast that is thine. His lord answered and said unto him, thou wicked and slothful servant, thou knewest that I reap where I sowed not, and gather where I have not strawed: Thou oughtest therefore to have put my money to the exchangers, and then at my coming I should have received mine own with usury. Take therefore the talent from him, and give it unto him which hath ten talents. For unto every one that hath shall be given, and he shall have abundance: but from him that hath not shall be taken away even that which he hath. And cast ye the unprofitable servant into outer darkness: there shall be weeping and gnashing of teeth. (Matthew 25:14-30)

God has given each of us at least one talent, to another God has given two, and to another more. Each of us has a talent, it is up to us to discover that talent. Jesus helps you discover the talent you have inside you. Then you refine and practice that talent. Then use it for the glory of God. Use it to bring souls into the Kingdom of God. By being a faithful manager, you increase the one talent into two. Look closely at what the man with one talent told the Lord. We must make sure we have no such words in us.

"Then he which had received the one talent came and said, Lord, I knew thee that thou art an hard man, reaping where thou hast not sown, and gathering where thou hast not strawed: And I was afraid, and went and hid thy talent in the earth: lo, there thou hast that is thine." (Vs. 24-25)

The wicked servant complained that life was very difficult, he found excuses for failure, he was not optimistic but he was pessimistic or negative about life. He was like the children of Israel who murmured and complained often about the Lord. Their hearts were not with the Lord.

Deep down inside of them, they loved the gods of the Egyptians, they despised their true identities, they preferred slavery over purpose and chose to place blame on God, instead of taking personal responsibility, having self-determination, self-discipline and trusting God to take them all the way through despite life's difficulties. They chose to be failures instead of winners. The wicked and unfaithful servant was called "unprofitable." One of the main reasons God invests in His children, other than the fact that He loves them, is that they are profitable. The wicked servant also said: "and I was afraid and went and hid thy talent." Fear will rob you of your true potential if you do not decide to overcome fear with love. Faith is the opposite of fear and faith works by love.

"For in Jesus Christ neither circumcision availeth anything, nor uncircumcision; but faith which worketh by love." (Galatians 5:6)

And love never fails:

"Love never fails..." ((1 Corinthians 13:8)

And God puts His love in our hearts:

> *"And not only so, but we glory in tribulations also: knowing that tribulation worketh patience; And patience, experience; and experience, hope: And hope maketh not ashamed; because the love of God is shed abroad in our hearts by the Holy Ghost which is given unto us." (Romans 5:3-5)*

So we are fully equipped to win! If you look at your circumstances they will discourage you. So don't look at them! The system is designed to demoralize because Satan invented the system of this world. Don't look at your situation, look at Jesus!

> *"Looking unto Jesus the author and finisher of our faith; who for the joy that was set before him endured the cross, despising the shame, and is set down at the right hand of the throne of God." (Hebrews 12:2)*

You look at Jesus by looking at what He says in his word. You keep your eyes and words on His promises, meditate on them and trust in Him completely. I do believe in giving to ministries if they are also in turn feeding, clothing, sheltering and educating the poor. But giving to the church does not multiply one's money. If that were the case, the investment banks of the world would be rushing to bring huge "financial seed" to churches so as to have their money multiplied. This doctrine has enriched many false prophets at the expense of simple Christians. Money is not multiplied by giving to the church. This is an incorrect business model for one's goals of financial freedom. The only reason a conman is able to take advantage of his victim is because the victim wants something for nothing! Money is NOT multiplied by simply giving it away. Money is multiplied by investment and entrepreneurship. If you give away all your money and wait for financial miracles to fall from Heaven, you will be disappointed. This has happened to many people and led to believers backsliding from Christianity. The truth is that your finances will change by your increase in knowledge and wisdom, also your ability to provide assistance and solve the problems of others. If you want to make money, the first thing you should do is STOP thinking about yourself and start thinking about what you can do for others as soon as possible.

> *"Through wisdom a house is built, And by understanding it is established; By knowledge the rooms are filled With all precious and pleasant riches." (Proverbs 24:3-4)*

Many Christians want to skip this stage altogether and simply give their money to the church and then sit at home waiting for financial miracles to fall from Heaven. Which loving father would only bless their child if the child gave him the last of their money? What kind of twisted love demands that the child first give to the parent before the parent can give to the child? Which heir, in the history of inheritance, had to give money to the owner of the will in order for the inheritance to be obtained? In these last days, those who do not know God's word will be made merchandise of. Meanwhile the pastors who dominate in the area of such doctrine buy themselves private jets and multimillion dollar mansions and splurge themselves with luxury cars all at the expense of financial seed sowers who are hoping for a financial shortcut from God. "Something for nothing," is the fool's understanding of how to get rich.

> *"Trust in the LORD with all your heart And do not lean on your own understanding. In all your ways acknowledge Him, And He will make your paths straight." (Proverbs 3:5-6)*

The whole bible is about God and His investment in mankind and how His investment has been over the years. God sending His son was an investment in the future of mankind. Yes! God has a vested interest in your future!

> *"For God so loved the world that He gave (invested) His only begotten son, that whosoever believes in*

him should not perish but have everlasting life." (John 3:16)

God's investment into humanity continues to do well even as over 2,000 years later Christianity is still growing and spreading at a rate which no other belief system can match. This brings us to a major point of wisdom we can see in God and if we are wise, we should emulate it. God does not invest in buildings, properties, assets, liabilities etc. although they are all good to have for us who live on the earth. He allows us to have those things and manage them for His Kingdom and for His glory.

But!

What God invests in is people. God is in the people business. People are His riches. You are the apple of His eye. The cream of the crop, a first fruits of His creatures. He is investing in you for the long term and He fully intends for His investment to bear much fruit and reap a bountiful harvest.

"Being confident of this very thing, that he which hath begun a good work in you will perform it until the day of Jesus Christ:" (Philippians 1:6)

"Be patient therefore, brethren, unto the coming of the Lord. Behold, the husbandman waiteth for the precious fruit of the earth, and hath long patience

for it, until he receive the early and latter rain." (James 5:7)

This life is your opportunity to bear much fruit and bring as much glory to God as possible. Everything we do in this world echoes in eternity. We can send shockwaves into the unseen realm by that which we choose to think and do while we are here. God is our biggest investor. Unfortunately, Satan is also an investor. His investments can be seen all over billboards which advertise alcohol, beer and ungodly lifestyles on television, the

internet, Hollywood, social media and cell phone contents. The more wealth Christians obtain, the more we can advertise Heaven. We can create our own movies, series, music and music videos. We can put up our own billboards advertising how much Jesus walks with us instead of Johnny Walker whiskey in our faces as we drive by on the highway. Remember something key which David the psalmist said:

"The LORD said unto my Lord, sit thou at my right hand, until I make thine enemies thy footstool." (Psalms 110:1)

The Father told our Lord Jesus Christ to sit at His right hand until He makes his enemies his footstool.

Guess who God is using to make the enemies of Jesus Christ his footstool?

Answer: You and me. It's up to us to take over and use every gift, talent and ability that God has given us to win souls for the Kingdom of God. We are God's ambassadors. We have not been sent into the world to live in defeat and then escape through some huge disappearing act. We have been sent to colonize the earth and occupy it until Jesus comes.

> *"And he called his ten servants, and delivered them ten pounds, and said unto them, occupy till I come." (Luke 19:13)*

We should be occupying until He, our Lord, comes. That's what the five wise maids did in Jesus' parable of the five wise virgins.

> *"Then shall the kingdom of heaven be likened unto ten virgins, which took their lamps, and went forth to meet the bridegroom. And five of them were wise, and five were foolish.*
>
> *They that were foolish took their lamps, and took no oil with them: But the wise took oil in their vessels with their lamps. While the bridegroom tarried, they all slumbered and slept.*
>
> *And at midnight there was a cry made, Behold, the bridegroom cometh; go ye out to meet Him. Then all those virgins arose, and trimmed their lamps. And the*

foolish said unto the wise, give us of your oil; for our lamps are gone out. But the wise answered, saying, not so; let there be not enough for us and you: but go ye rather to them that sell, and buy for yourselves. And while they went to buy, the bridegroom came; and they that were ready went in with him to the marriage: and the door was shut. Afterward came also the other virgins, saying, Lord, Lord, open to us. 12 But he answered and said, Verily I say unto you,

I know you not. Watch therefore, for ye know neither the day nor the hour wherein the Son of man cometh." (Matthew 25:1-13)

The oil in the lamps of the five wise virgins represents anointing.

"But my horn shalt thou exalt like the horn of an unicorn: I shall be anointed with fresh oil." (Psalms 92:10)

Now the anointing is that which breaks the yoke of slavery. It is not possible to speak about money in this world without speaking on slavery because when man does not know his identity, he becomes a slave, and a slave will be paid a slave's wages. Jesus gives you your true identity, without Jesus, you cannot know your purpose, working for money becomes your purpose, which reduces you to a slave, if that is all you are here for. This slavery becomes your endless cycle. But the anointing of teaching begins to deprogram the slave's mind which has been raised, trained from childhood, and reprogram you with the King's mind. That's why Philippians 5:2 says:

> *"Let this mind be in you, which was also in Christ Jesus:" Romans 12:2 says:*

> *"And do not be conformed to this world, but be transformed by the renewing of your mind,"*

The process of becoming a winner in Christ is the process of renewing your mind continuously.

Until when, you may ask?

Until Christ be formed in you!

> *"My little children, of whom I travail in birth again until Christ be formed in you" (Galatians 4:19)*

Those who mature in the faith come into their inheritance spoken of in Galatians 4:1,

> *"Now I say, as long as the heir is a child, he does not differ at all from a slave although he is owner of everything, 2but he is under guardians and*

managers until the date set by the father. 3So also we, while we were children, were held in bondage under the elemental things of the world."

This scripture tells us that while we were slaves, we were considered to be children under bondage. Those in bondage serve because they are forced to. But those of us with freedom serve the Lord out of gladness and joy. Before you obtain your inheritance, you are taught and instructed on how to obtain your inheritance. Then once you are set free from yourself , (your old way of thinking), you proceed to fulfill destiny.

"The backslider in heart shall be filled with his own ways: and a good man shall be satisfied from himself." (Proverbs 14:1)

To be satisfied from yourself is to put off the old man and be completely renewed in the spirit of your mind. But many Christians get stuck at the first stages of salvation. So when the world sees them, they see no difference between themselves and those who claim to be saved. Beloved, this should not be so. You are supposed to be maturing and growing. Your situation should be improving:

"But the path of the just is as the shining light, that shineth more and more unto the perfect day." (Proverbs 4:18)

One grows in grace, through growing in the knowledge of the Lord Jesus Christ. That means growing in knowledge of the word of God.

> *"Grace and peace be multiplied unto you through the knowledge of God, and of Jesus our Lord," (2 Peter 1:2)*

So the grace on your life can grow and with it, your influence, your affluence, your anointing, etc. can and should increase. This is your ministry, the fulfillment of your destiny and the working out of your purpose. Remember, I told you that when an eagle is flying, it is working. When a fish is swimming, it is working. When you are working, that is not slavery. It's the fulfillment of purpose. It's personal leadership. It is living by example. It is doing what God created you to do without being financially exploited or being forced to compromise your integrity in exchange for making a living. Work is one of the first things God gave Adam and it was never a curse. God never cursed Adam, God cursed the ground.

> *"And unto Adam he said, because thou hast hearkened unto the voice of thy wife, and hast eaten of the tree, of which I commanded thee, saying, thou shalt not eat of it: cursed is the ground for thy sake; in sorrow shalt thou eat of it all the days of thy life;*

Thorns also and thistles shall it bring forth to thee; and thou shalt eat the herb of the field;" (Genesis 3:17-18)

The thorns and thistles were worn on Jesus' head when He was crucified. He took away the evil harvest which man would be forced to reap as a result of sowing (investing) seeds of sin. He took our evil harvest which we should have reaped for our actions (which is slavery) As soon as you sinned, the spirit realm was very well aware. The punishment for your sin was handwritten on your forehead. That was slavery, suffering and punishment programmed into your life as payment for missing the mark, written on your forehead. But Jesus wiped that handwriting away with his blood on the cross.

"Blotting out the handwriting of ordinances that was against us, which was contrary to us, and took it out of the way, nailing it to his cross." (Colossians 2:14)

I like the New American Standard Version's rendering of this verse:

"Having canceled out the certificate of debt consisting of decrees against us, which was hostile to us; and He has taken it out of the way, having nailed it to the cross." (Colossians 2:14)

This is why you can succeed and not just survive but thrive! The memory of your old sins can be washed away and replaced by new memories of God's word and His promises to you.

> *"How much more will the blood of Christ, who through the eternal Spirit offered Himself without blemish to God, cleanse your conscience from dead works to serve the living God? (Hebrews 9:14 - NASB)*

Shame and self-condemnation causes people to see themselves as less than how God sees them. Shame will affect your performance; the same way your performance would be different if you stood naked in front of people as opposed to standing fully clothed. Shame has a powerful negative effect on your everyday life. But once the blood of Jesus washes those sins away, there is no more need for shame because God does not condemn you. And if God does not condemn you, nobody can.

> *"There is therefore now no condemnation to them which are in Christ Jesus, who walk not after the flesh, but after the Spirit." (Romans 8:1)*

Finally, our lifelong investments into the Kingdom of God will one day bring returns. We may not know what kind of returns we can expect while in this world, but we know that if we keep our lamps filled with oil, the returns will be glorious! Imagine the souls who will come to Christ because of your testimony. Imagine the change you are making in the lives of others as they watch your life. You are a living testimony that Jesus is real and that He is alive. Our entire lives should be viewed as an investment into the Kingdom of God. Investments are made with the foresight that it will be possible in the future to make a profit. We are giving our lives as living sacrifices unto our Heavenly Father. Investing our physical mortal bodies in hope of invincible eternal bodies.

> *"For this perishable must put on the imperishable, and this mortal must put on immortality." (1 Corinthians 15:53 - NASB)*

The investment of this life, in exchange for eternal life is an extraordinary opportunity for God to separate those who will serve Him from those who will not. The manifold wisdom of God in allowing mankind to pass through this time of testing, is to separate those who are His, from those who are not. Life in this world is one big process of elimination. He is sifting out His own from those children of Satan who are not His own. Satan has children of his own as well. We have already touched on the 13 satanic bloodlines in this publication. They have been in positions of power for centuries. I will release more publications on those bloodlines as the Lord directs. But now it is time for the intercessors and prayer warriors to begin praying in opposition to these families and more specifically to prayerfully bring down their financial dominance in this world. Their banking families have the right to print and lend money to the children of Satan and those who are not saved. But they have no right to print and lend money to the body of Christ. For we are Abraham's seed, and our Father gave us clear instructions concerning lending and borrowing. He said,

> *"For the LORD your God will bless you as he has promised, and you will lend to many nations but will borrow from none. You will rule over many nations but none will rule over you." (Deuteronomy 15:6)*

This is the commandment and the promise we have received from our Heavenly Father. Our loyalty is to him and not to men. We will keep His statutes and walk in His ways. We are His children and the sheep of His pasture. Our fulfillment in life comes from serving and living for Him. Therefore, this current banking system of wickedness is unacceptable and as it was prophesied by the prophet Ezekiel, it will collapse and the dead bones who were the children of Israel will live again. Modern day capitalism began on the backs of Hebrew slaves. This is the truth about money. Hebrews in Africa and all over the world are beginning to wake up to their true identity. The dividing of the African continent was done so by European powers for the exploitation of human and natural resources and also to cover the identity of who the Hebrew people are as well as to wipe out the heritage of Godly righteousness from the face of the earth forever.

> *"Keep not thou silence, O God: hold not thy peace, and be not still, O God. For, lo, thine enemies make a tumult: and they that hate thee have lifted up the head. They have taken crafty counsel against thy people, and consulted against thy hidden ones. They have said, Come, and let us cut them off from being a nation; that the name of Israel may be no more in remembrance. For they have consulted together with one consent: they are confederate against thee: The tabernacles of Edom, and the Ishmaelites; of Moab, and the Hagarenes;" (Psalms 83:1-6)*

This is the biggest secret. The true identity of the real children of Israel. This is part of the secrets of Freemasonry. This hidden truth is so explosive it has the power to awaken the lost tribes and cause them to call upon the name of the Lord Jesus saying, "Blessed is he that comes in the name of the Lord! The Hebrews will begin to wake up and realize who they are all over the world and the gospel will be preached like it has never been preached and the power of God will pour out like the world has never seen it. These are exciting times to be alive. I pray that this publication and other publications like it will continue to open the eyes of Christians and nonbelievers alike, all over the world and prepare the way for the coming of the Lord.

> *"When the Son of man shall come in his glory, and all the holy angels with him, then shall he sit upon the throne of his glory: And before him shall be gathered all nations: and he shall separate them one from another, as a shepherd divideth his sheep from the goats: And he shall set the sheep on his right hand, but the goats on the left. Then shall the King say unto them on his right hand, Come, ye blessed of my Father, inherit the kingdom prepared for you from the foundation of the world: For I was an hungred, and ye gave me meat: I was thirsty, and ye gave me drink: I was a stranger, and ye took me in: Naked, and ye clothed me: I was sick, and ye visited me: I was in prison, and ye came unto me. Then shall the righteous answer him, saying, Lord, when saw we thee an hungred, and fed thee? or thirsty, and gave thee drink? When saw we thee a stranger, and took thee in? or naked, and clothed thee? Or when saw we thee sick, or in prison, and came unto thee? And the King shall answer and say unto them, Verily I*

say unto you, inasmuch as ye have done it unto one of the least of these my brethren, ye have done it unto me. Then shall he say also unto them on the left hand, depart from me, ye cursed, into everlasting fire, prepared for the devil and his angels: For I was an hungred, and ye gave me no meat: I was thirsty, and ye gave me no drink: I was a stranger, and ye took me not in: naked, and ye clothed me not: sick, and in prison, and ye visited me not. Then shall they also answer him, saying, Lord, when saw we thee an hungred, or athirst, or a stranger, or naked, or sick, or in prison, and did not minister unto thee? Then shall he answer them, saying, Verily I say unto you, inasmuch as ye did it not to one of the least of these, ye did it not to me. And these shall go away into everlasting punishment: but the righteous into life eternal." (Matthew 25:31-46)

CHAPTER TEN

The Principles of Poverty

The following is a list of principles which the poor must obey in order for poverty to thrive. Nobody wants to be poor, yet at one time or another we have all made poor financial decisions in our lives.

Let us first define poverty. Poverty is a multifaceted concept, which may include social, economic, and political elements. Absolute poverty, extreme poverty, or destitution refers to the complete lack of the means necessary to meet basic personal needs such as food, clothing and shelter.

Poverty is also the inability to produce. Poverty, like any other state of existence in the world, has principles.

Those who obey its principles will have poverty enough. As you go through this list, having made poverty an enemy, see if there is anything which you are doing to allow poverty to remain in your life. Then train yourself to do the opposite. You will find that poverty will soon feel too uncomfortable to stay with you. Having found you to be an unaccommodating host, it will leave. You find that amazingly, poverty as a state of being, requires the complete cooperation of the host, in order to remain and thrive. There are more principles of poverty than the ones listed below, but the idea of not cooperating with the principles of poverty is what I intend to convey. Therefore, in order for poverty to continue in your life, it makes the following suggestions: (I have added the corresponding scripture references on financial wisdom below each poverty point for your convenience).

You can thank me later!

Do not make your money make money for you. In other words, do not invest. Hope to just get a job somewhere by luck and survive! *"And that ye study to be quiet, and to do your own business, and to work with your own hands, as we commanded you;" (1Thessalonians 4:11)*

Do not start your own business. Refuse to be an entrepreneur and put all your hopes in employment.

Put your full trust in job security (employment) and save for a pension! *"Invest in seven ventures, yes, in eight; you do not know what disaster may come upon the land." (Ecclesiastes 11:2)*

Do not learn the laws and principles of money. Keep believing that money is not for you, it's only for those born in rich families, not for people like you. *"For God hath not given us the spirit of fear; but of power, and of love, and of a sound* *mind." (2 Timothy 1:7)*

Do not learn how to be an entrepreneur. Assume that just because you are an A student you will be a success in life. Do not learn other skills, only rely on your academic ability. *"The wise of heart will receive commands, But a babbling fool will be ruined." (Proverbs 10:8 KJV)*

Do not make passive income. *"And thou shalt have goats' milk enough for thy food, for the food of thy household, and for the maintenance for thy maidens." (*Proverbs 27:27 *KJV)*

Give all your money to churches and expect miracle money to fall from heaven. *"And through covetousness shall they with feigned words make merchandise of you: whose judgment now of a long time lingereth not, and their damnation slumbereth not." (2 Peter 2:3 KJV)*

Do not read books or educate yourself on your own. Believe that you already know everything and since you finished school, there's nothing else to be learned! *"The lips of the righteous feed many: but fools die for want of wisdom." (Proverbs 10:21)*

Do not learn about the stock market or the securities exchange markets. Say such things as 'such things are not my cup of tea." *"Wisdom is too high for fools; in the assembly at* *the gate they must not open their mouths." (Proverbs 24:7)*

Do not learn the difference between assets and liabilities. *"A hypocrite with his mouth destroyeth his neighbor: but through knowledge shall the just be delivered."* (Proverbs 11:9)

Invest in liabilities. *"He who observes the wind will not sow, And he who regards the clouds will not reap." (Ecclesiastes 11:4)*

Do not invest in assets. *"Where no oxen are, the crib is clean: but much increase is by the strength of the ox." (Proverbs 14:4)*

Focus on buying instead of selling. Go shopping all the time! Always dream about what you want to buy! Picture yourself buying everything you could possibly imagine! *"Through wisdom a house is built, and by understanding it is established; By knowledge the rooms are filled with all precious and pleasant riches." (Proverbs 24:3-4)*

Do not learn about or invest in real estate. Don't worry about construction, let others learn those things. Building is boring. *"Therefore everyone who hears these words of Mine and acts on them, may be compared to a wise man who built his house on the rock." (Matthew 7:24)*

Take drugs and alcohol. As soon as Friday is here, party hard! You only live once (YOLO)! *"Give strong drink to him who is perishing, and wine to him whose life is bitter." (Proverbs 31:6)*

Do not have a financial mentor. Be envious of those doing well. After all, who do they think they are to be doing better than you? *"Mark the perfect man, and behold the upright: for the end of that man is peace." (Psalms 37:37)*

Rely on other people like brokers and financial salesmen or politicians to secure your financial future. After all, is it not the job of the government to secure my future? *"Thus saith the LORD; Cursed be the man that trusteth in man, and maketh flesh his arm, and whose heart departeth from the LORD." (Jeremiah 17:5)*

Fill your mind with secular hip-hop, trap, rock, reggae, and party music. After all, music is life right?

"For the one who sows to his own flesh will from the flesh reap corruption, but the one who sows to the Spirit will from the Spirit reap eternal life."(Galatians 6:8 NASB)

Hang out and spend time with other poor people. *"He that walketh with wise men shall be wise: but a companion of fools shall be destroyed." (Proverbs 13:20 KJV)*

Do not take calculated financial risks. Play it safe all the time. Do not invest, fear losing money more than making it. *"Invest in seven ventures, yes, in eight; you do not know what disaster may come upon the land." (Ecclesiastes 11:2)*

Do not have a team, work alone and be greedy. Nowadays you can't trust anyone. Do everything by yourself, keep all the money, and do not give anyone anything, ever! *"The liberal soul shall be made fat: and he that watereth shall be watered also himself." (Proverbs 11:25)*

Marry a golddigger. They may love you for your money, but at least they're cute! *"The wise woman builds her house, But the foolish tears it down with her own hands."* (Proverbs 14:1) **AND** *"Let thy fountain be blessed: and rejoice with the wife of thy youth." (Proverbs 5:18)*

Do not be a man/woman of your word. Do not pay debts on time. Be undependable and unpredictable.

"A good name is rather to be chosen than great riches, and loving favour rather than silver and gold." *(Proverbs 22:1)*

Be afraid, be very afraid. Too afraid to do anything. *"The sluggard says, "There is a lion outside; I will be killed in the streets!" (Proverbs 22:13)*

Do not give to the poor, but despise them. "*He that*

oppresseth the poor reproacheth his Maker: but he that honoreth him hath mercy on the poor." (Proverbs 14:31)

Spend all your free time watching TV. Especially now that Netflix has all your favorite shows, splurge and binge watch all night! *"The hand of the diligent shall bear rule: but the slothful shall be under tribute." (Proverbs 12:24*

Get into debt. Then borrow more money to pay off your previous creditor. Rob Peter to pay Paul.

"He that is surety for a stranger shall smart for it: and he that hateth suretiship is sure." (Proverbs 11:15) **AND "***Owe no one anything except to love one another, for he who loves another has fulfilled the law. (Romans 13:8)*

Participate in "instant gratification." *As soon as you have enough money to buy a car, buy it. Impress your friends who are broke anyway. The world must know who you are! "Pride goeth before destruction, and an haughty spirit before a fall." (Proverbs 16:18)*

Use credit cards and shop till you drop! *"For Jehovah thy God will bless thee, as he promised thee: and thou shalt lend unto many nations, but thou shalt not borrow; and thou shalt rule over many nations, but they shall not rule over thee." (Deuteronomy 15:6)*

Over invest in beautification. Fake nails, fake hair, fake weaves, fake everything! Nowadays everyone gets a little work on their face done. Get some Botox, liposuction for that fat belly and throw in some weight loss pills.

You don't have to exercise to lose weight, just pop pills! Get breast implants and butt jobs, the bigger the better!

"Favour is deceitful, and beauty is vain: but a woman that feareth the LORD, she shall be praised." (Proverbs 31:30)

Impulse purchase. If you see it, you like it, buy it! Now! Do not give yourself two weeks to actually think about whether you need this thing right now or not. *"Be still before the Lord and wait patiently for him;* do not fret when people succeed in their ways, when they carry out their wicked schemes" (Psalms 37:7 NIV)

Waste food and eat out everyday. *"Much food is in the tillage of the poor: but there is that which is destroyed for want of judgment." (Proverbs 13:23)*

Purchase lucky talismans, charms, crosses, chains, anointing oil, prayer shawls, blessed virgin statues, etc. while reciting incantations and confessions, you may need the blessings of the ancestors in order to obtain financial blessings as well. Perform financial rituals or give large sums of money to churches as financial seed. Then wait for the miracle money to come rolling in! *"Thus saith the LORD, thy redeemer, and he that formed thee from the womb, I am the LORD that maketh all things; that stretcheth forth the heavens alone; that spreadeth abroad the earth by myself; that frustrateth the tokens of the liars, and maketh diviners mad; that turneth wise men backward, and maketh their knowledge foolish;" (Isaiah 44:24-25)*

Health (ignoring symptoms will make you better) Don't do any check ups and don't exercise! *"For physical training is of some value, but godliness has value for all things, holding promise for both the present life and the life to come." (1 Timothy 4:8)*

Buy video games and play them all day! *"The soul of the sluggard desireth, and hath nothing: but the soul of the diligent shall be made fat." (Proverbs 13:4)*

Gamble, play lottery, lotto, roll dice, go to the casino and try your luck etc. Hope to win money instead of earning it. *"Those who want to get rich fall into temptation and a trap and into many foolish and harmful desires that plunge people into ruin and destruction. For the love of money is a root of all kinds of evil. Some people, eager for money, have wandered from the faith and pierced themselves with many griefs." (Timothy 6:9-10)* AND *"The greedy bring ruin to their households but the* *one who hates bribes will win." (Proverbs 15:27)*

Pay more taxes! *"The hand of the diligent shall bear rule: but the slothful shall be under tribute." (Proverbs 12:24)*

Give your money to pastors who promise a 30, 60, 100 fold return to fall from heaven. The more famous or anointed they say they are, the more money will fall from Heaven! *"And through covetousness shall they with feigned words make merchandise of you: whose judgment now of a long time lingereth not, and their damnation slumbereth not." They promise them freedom, while they themselves are slaves of depravity–for "people are slaves to whatever has mastered them." (2 Peter 2:19)*

Assume that the rich are all evil. Since there's no way to get rich in the world except stealing and since you have never stolen you are far better than them. *"He that is despised, and hath a servant, is better than he that honoureth himself, and lacketh bread." (Proverbs 12:9)*

Continuously miss out on opportunities. Never be at the right place at the right time with the right people.

P.O.O.R. is also an acronym, Passing Over Opportunities Repeatedly! *"I have seen something else under the sun: The race is not to the swift or the battle to the strong, nor does food come to the wise or wealth to the brilliant or favor to the* *learned; but time and chance happen to them all." (Ecclesiastes 9:11)*

Be inconsistent. If it doesn't work the first time, just forget about it. It wasn't meant to be. *"The hand of the diligent shall bear rule: but the slothful shall be under tribute." (Proverbs 12:24)*

Sleep all day! Go ahead, dream as much as possible, don't let the sun interrupt your snooze time. Every time your cell phone alarm goes off hit the snooze button! "*Yet a little sleep, a little slumber, a little folding of the hands to sleep: So shall thy poverty come as one that travelleth; and thy want as an armed man." (Proverbs 24:33,34)*

This is just a short list of the things which rob us of possibilities every day. Can you think of any more? Write them down and print them out and then place them on your wall. Train yourself to avoid obeying the principles of poverty.

Chapter Eleven

A Rich Mindset

Success is said to be the sum of small positive actions repeated consistently for extended periods of time. Money comes from solving other people's problems and making their lives easier. Look around your world, do you see any problems? Can you think of solutions to these problems? If you're in a third world country, look at how people in America and Europe have solved some of their problems. See if those solutions have been implemented locally. If not, be the first to do it! Start finding out how you can solve those problems, even if it will take years, the time spent learning will make you very rich!

The rich mindset is a problem solving mindset. A millionaire's mind is very productive. Even if you took his money away, within a short time his money would return, because of his mindset and the things he has learned over time. Conversely, if you gave millions to a poor man, chances are, within a short time he would be poor again. Because his mind is poor and only thinks of himself, his financial circumference will reduce from the size of millions, back to the size he was before he received the money. This is why it is said, "if you give a man a fish, he eats for a day, but if you teach a man to fish, he can eat every day," and might I add, "he can teach others, open a fishing school, export fish and improve the economy."

I noticed something about rich people. The rich take advice from people they admire, the poor take advice from people they trust or have been told to trust. Learning is a continuous process, the earlier you start, the better off your life will be. Learn from people who do what they teach. If you want to be rich, do not learn exclusively from employees because they can only teach you how to be an employee (like university and college professors). Men often have the problem of ego. They think they know everything. Again, the problem with pride is that it does not take into account what it does not know. Most professors in universities are broke, yet they teach economics. The irony! If they understood how to make money work for them, they would not be working for money. Do today what others will not, so that you can do tomorrow, what others cannot. This discipline will separate you from the masses and put you in a class of your own. The "problem havers" are the vast majority of the world's population and are overcrowded. The "problem solvers" are few and far between. There is plenty of room at the millionaires and billionaires table for problem solvers. This publication was designed to help solve the problem of financial education, financial intelligence and identity crisis. Christ solves the problem of identity; financial education is a journey you must now commence or continue if you had already started. A financially stable Christian is far less likely to compromise their integrity in exchange for money. Jesus said something very interesting to his disciples in Luke 16:1-13,

> *"And he said also unto his disciples, there was a certain rich man, which had a steward; and the same was accused unto him that he had wasted his goods. And he called him, and said unto him, how is it that I hear this of thee? give an account of thy stewardship; for thou mayest be no longer steward. Then the steward said within himself, what shall I do? for my lord taketh away from me the stewardship: I cannot dig; to beg I am ashamed.*
>
> *I am resolved what to do, that, when I am put out of the stewardship, they may receive me into their houses. So he called every one of his lord's debtors unto him, and said unto the first, How much owest thou unto my lord? And he said, An hundred measures of oil. And he said unto him, Take thy bill, and sit down quickly, and write fifty. Then said he to another,*

And how much owest thou? And he said, An hundred measures of wheat. And he said unto him, Take thy bill, and write fourscore. And the lord commended the unjust steward, because he had done wisely: for the children of this world are in their generation wiser than the children of light. And I say unto you, make to yourselves friends of the mammon of unrighteousness; that, when ye fail, they may receive you into everlasting habitations.He that is faithful in that which is least is faithful also in much: and he that is unjust in the least is unjust also in much. If therefore ye have not been faithful in the unrighteous mammon, who will commit to your trust the true riches? And if ye have not been faithful in that which is another man's, who shall give you that which is your own? No servant can serve two masters: for either he will hate the one, and love the other; or else he will hold to the one, and despise the other. Ye cannot serve God and mammon."

The unjust steward's ability to think ahead is what Jesus called "the wisdom of the children of this world." It is the wisdom of planning ahead for inevitabilities. Jesus commanded his disciples to "make friends of the mammon of unrighteousness, that when you fail, they may receive you into everlasting habitations." In other words, learn how to prepare for hard times during the good times. So that you won't have hard times when others are having hard times. This is a path to wealth acquisition. In the city of the blind, the one eyed man is king. The man who knows what is coming is prepared, he is self-disciplined, he knows that others do not know what he knows. Inside information can make you very wealthy. If you are faithful in preparing with small steps every day over time, then you can be trusted with huge amounts of wealth when times of hardship arrive.

The Federal Reserve is a privately owned banking institution which increases and decreases the money supply to create "booms" and "busts," in the market in order to suck all of the world's human and natural resources into the hands of a few dominant families. With that knowledge, one can prepare in the "boom" times for the next "bust." In Genesis 41 starting at verse one we read about Pharaoh's dream. In his dream he elaborated how he saw seven fat cows followed by seven thin starving cows which in turn devoured the seven fat cows and still remained thin. Then he woke up. Then after falling asleep the second time he saw in his dream seven ears of corn came upon the stalk, fat and healthy. Then seven thin ears, blasted with the east wind, sprung up after them, and the seven thin ears devoured the seven fat and healthy ears and then he woke up and realized it was a dream. Pharaoh then sent for his wise men, his brokers, his magicians, his estate and financial planners to explain the meaning of the dream but no one could. Then Pharaoh's butler told him about Joseph, who's dream interpretation gift had helped him before. Pharaoh sent for Joseph immediately and they brought him up out of the prison in haste and presented him before Pharaoh. Pharaoh explains the dream to Joseph and Joseph is careful to tell Pharaoh that it is God, the giver of gifts who will give Pharaoh an answer of peace. Then Joseph tells Pharaoh that the dream is one and that God is showing Pharaoh what He is about to do. The seven good cows were seven good years of plenty throughout the land of Egypt, the seven thin cows were to be seven years of profound famine so severe that the seven years of plenty would be forgotten. Therefore, Joseph as a wise estate planner explained that Pharaoh should take a fifth of all of the land of Egypt to plant and save food and store it in giant stores in preparation for the seven years of severe famine. Then Pharaoh says something very interesting in the 38th verse of chapter 41.

> *"And Pharaoh said unto his servants, can we find such a one as this is, a man in whom the spirit of God is? (Genesis 41:38)*

Pharaoh then proceeded to make Joseph the prime minister of Egypt, setting him over all the land of Egypt. Pharaoh noticed that the Spirit of God was a spirit of wisdom and foresight. This same Spirit is given unto every born again believer. Only Pharaoh had authority over Joseph, nobody else. Joseph now had the responsibility of aggressively farming, harvesting and storing food. Then in Genesis 41:49 it says:

> *"And Joseph gathered corn as the sand of the sea, very much, until he left numbering; for it was without number."*

So after the years of plenty came the years of famine. After one year of famine the Egyptians came to Pharaoh begging for food. Pharaoh sent them to Joseph who opened the storehouses and began selling food to the Egyptians. The whole world was so dry because of the famine that they all came to Egypt for food. Thus the wisdom which God gave to Joseph put him in a position to sell food to the whole world and save them from starvation. The wisdom of Joseph should be emulated by every Christian. During the good years he saved and prepared for the bad years to come. During the good years commodities were in large supply and short demand. This lowered the price of the food. During this time Joseph stored as much food as possible. Then during the famine the price of food began to increase exponentially. Demand for food had skyrocketed while supply was now short. Genesis 47 from verse 13 tells us:

"And there was no bread in all the land; for the famine was very sore, so that the land of Egypt and all the land of Canaan fainted by reason of the famine. And Joseph gathered up all the money that was found in the land of Egypt, and in the land of Canaan, for the corn which they bought: and Joseph brought the money into Pharaoh's house. And when money failed in the land of Egypt, and in the land of Canaan, all the Egyptians came unto Joseph, and said, Give us bread: for why should we die in thy presence? for the money faileth. And Joseph said, give your cattle; and I will give you for your cattle, if money fail. And they brought their cattle unto Joseph: and Joseph gave them bread in exchange for horses, and for the flocks, and for the cattle of the herds, and for the asses: and he fed them with bread for all their cattle for that year. When that year was ended, they came unto him the second year, and said unto him, We will not hide it from my lord, how that our money is spent; my lord also hath our herds of cattle; there is not ought left in the sight of my lord, but our bodies, and our lands: Wherefore shall we die before thine eyes, both we and our land? buy us and our land for bread, and we and our land will be servants unto Pharaoh: and give us seed, that we

may live, and not die, that the land be not desolate.

And Joseph bought all the land of Egypt for Pharaoh; for the Egyptians sold every man his field, because the famine prevailed over them: so the land became Pharaoh's."

Because of the foresight of Joseph, Pharaoh was able to purchase everything in Egypt including the Egyptians themselves. Here is a powerful principle in wealth acquisition. He who knows the future and prepares for it will rule over those who do not. Foresight made Pharaoh the richest man in the world because they prepared while everyone else was throwing parties and having a good time during the years of plenty. This was a classic "Boom" and "bust" scenario. The boom years were the years of plenty while the bust years were the years of famine.

Principle: The disciplined will rule over the indisciplined and the prepared will rule over the unprepared.

The followers of Christ are called disciples. A disciple is a disciplined one. Jesus is preparing us for dominion. Discipline and foresight are prerequisites for dominion. Dominion is one of the first commandments of God.

"And God blessed them, and God said unto them, be fruitful, and multiply, and replenish the earth,

and subdue it: and have DOMINION over the fish of the sea, and over the fowl of the air, and over every living thing that moveth upon the earth." (Genesis 1:28)

Just before the U.S. housing boom ended in 2007, investment firms were flourishing. Very few were prepared for the coming bust. Lehman Brothers, which Fortune magazine had called the number one most admired securities firm in 2007 filed for bankruptcy just one year later with $639 billion dollars in assets and $619 billion USD in debt. Lehman's bankruptcy filing was the largest in history. Lehman's failure to prepare during the boom years left it vulnerable at the very beginning of the bust. Again, through "booms" and "busts" the banking institutions will end up owning everything because they're able to prepare. It appears as if ever since Egypt's boom and bust with Joseph at the center, Satan has decided to copy, pervert and replicate what God did at that time in order to bring all of the world's resources both human and natural under his ownership. It appears Satan's financial policy is; "through booms and busts, own everything."

From the year 2000 until 2007 were boom years. The following years have been spent in recovery from the "Great Depression" of 2007/2008. The keen Christian should now take advantage of this useful wisdom and prepare for the next bust during the boom years. During the bust years everything was cheaper. That is the time to buy. During the boom years everything is more expensive, that is the time to sell. Like Joseph did. The times when prices are going up are called the "bull markets." The times when prices are going down are called the "bear markets." Obviously, in order to turn a profit, one should buy low and sell high for capital gains. It is also possible to make money in a bear market by knowing ahead of time that prices are about to go down, and then borrowing stock and selling it immediately in anticipation of the downturn. Then when the price goes down, buy the stock again and return it from where you borrowed it and keep the difference. This is how "bears" make money in a down market.

The whole Christian life is about preparing now for that which is coming tomorrow. The word of God is 2/3rds prophecy. We have seen how prophets foretold the transatlantic and (Hebrew) slave trade. God's word foretold the occupation of Israel by gentiles as it is now.

> *"But woe unto them that are with child, and to them that give suck, in those days! for there shall be great distress in the land, and wrath upon this people. And they shall fall by the edge of the sword, and shall be led away captive into all nations: and Jerusalem shall be trodden down of the Gentiles, until the times*

of the Gentiles be fulfilled." (Luke 21:23)

Just as Jesus foretold, Jerusalem was invaded by Rome in 70 AD. Over the following years the Hebrews were then scattered and taken captive into "all nations' where they were made slaves with no identity and no history or heritage since it was taken away from them by their captors. Even their biblical names were taken from them. They forgot who they were and whose they were. The Bible's accuracy in previous prophecies should be enough to let you know that it is very dependable. If the Bible foretells it, we can bank on it. Life after death is foretold in the word of God. Have you made investments in this life in preparation for the next?

In order to escape the "prison financial system" called Capitalism, you must have a plan. That should be your first step!

Write down a plan. "*For which of you, intending to build a tower, sitteth not down first, and counteth the cost, whether he have sufficient to finish it?" (Luke 14:28)* Planning is finishing before you begin. Planning is the premeditated, preconceived allocation of how resources will be used before they are used.

During the forming of the privately owned Federal Reserve Bank (which is NOT Federal and neither does it have any Reserves), the richest people in the world gathered and planned how to take control of the richest country in the world and then they changed the rules of money. A perpetual robbery is taking place in America and around the world (by default) as the people go to work in the businesses of the rich, save money in the banks of the rich, and invest in the assets of the rich (stocks, mutual funds and bonds) through the investment bankers to the rich. The system is designed to take as much of your money as possible, legally. Part of your financial plan for Godly financial management should be:

- Improving your financial understanding
- Protecting your money
- Budgeting your money
- Leveraging your money
- Improving your financial information

Get out of debt and stay out. One of your most powerful wealth building tools is your income. If it is being deducted because of debt you are doing yourself a disservice. The worst kind of debt one can possibly get into is a car-loan. This is because you will end up paying almost two times what the car is actually worth to the bank and you are paying for a liability which will decrease in value as soon as you drive it off the car lot by 30%. This is a liability which is losing value and costing you money. Taking a loan for a liability is one of the principles of poverty. It is not financially intelligent to do so, you will have violated the law of delayed gratification.

Live on far less than you make. Some people get a raise in salary at their job and immediately move into a bigger house. This is a lack of financial intelligence since their expenses have now increased and their asset column has not. So basically they are not in any better position than they were before the promotion. This mistake is made by many who have something to prove to others instead of first of all proving something to themselves. *"The wise man saves for the future, but the foolish man spends whatever he gets." (Proverbs 21:20)* Living on less than you make allows you to pay yourself more and invest in high performance assets.

Invest in assets not liabilities. The financial intelligence of this step cannot be overemphasized. Most people who start making money get lost at step 3. They start assuming they're rich and get lost along the way.

Form a corporation as soon as possible. Preferably a Limited liability Company (LLC). This will allow you to make money (from your assets), then spend money and then pay taxes. Instead of the other way around which is experienced by employees who get taxed first and then make the rest and then spend what's left over.

In other words, corporations:

a. make money

b. spend money

c. pay tax on profits

Meanwhile employees:

a. make money

b. pay taxes before they are even paid since it is deducted from their salaries first and then

c. spend money (on bills, expenses, food, clothing & shelter etc.)

Learning the process of forming a corporation will sharpen your entrepreneurial skills and push you into the world of business. The wisdom you acquire through this process will be worth everything you go through since this is the path to financial freedom.

The key here is simply a difference in mindset. The poor and middle class work for a paycheck. The rich work to acquire assets which send cash flow their way on a daily basis. The fundamental difference between these two ways of thinking concerning work separates the poor man from the rich man.

These are some of the vital lessons I learned during my years in the United States meeting with wealthy people, some of whom are famous, some are not. You may have started poor, I did too, but it does not mean you have to stay there. With the wisdom of God and strong desire to improve your life I can guarantee you one thing. Your tomorrow will be far greater than today.

CHAPTER TWELVE

Let Us Pray

By now it should be very clear to you that Satan, working closely with his children and their blind followers dominate global economics through international banking. The only group I know on the earth that can put a stop to Satan's operations is the body of Christ. The only reason why Satan has been able to get this far with his families and his privately owned central banks is because Christians have largely been in the dark about these issues. "Jesus is coming to take us all away, so why bother with the affairs of the earth?" is how some Christians feel about this topic. But what they are not taking into consideration is that if we have the power to stop Satan in his tracks concerning anything, we should do it. No questions asked. (Moreover, it won't hurt to try!)

> *"Truly I say to you, whatever you bind on earth shall have been bound in heaven; and whatever you loose on earth shall have been loosed in heaven. Again I say to you, that if two of you agree on earth about anything that they may ask, it shall be done for them by My Father who is in heaven. For where two or*

three have gathered together in My name, I am there in their midst." (Matthew 18:18-20)

This gives us great authority on the face of the earth. Read this!

"I will give you the keys of the kingdom of heaven; and whatever you bind on earth shall have been bound in heaven, and whatever you loose on earth shall have been loosed in heaven." (Matthew 16:19)

Jesus words' let us know that the body of Christ plays a major role in what is allowed to happen in the world and what is not (within certain parameters). We can petition the Father that He bring an end to certain satanic operations. Even if they are not stopped immediately, we will have set the ball rolling.

"Whatsoever we ask in Jesus' name will be done, that the Father may be glorified in the son."

(John 14:13)

With those few words, please agree with me as our church prays the following prayer. Your amen as a believer will be accepted in Heaven and counted.

"Father in the name of Jesus, We, your children, thank you for your word, for sending Jesus and for the power of attorney we have been given to use His mighty name. We thank you that whenever 2 or 3 of us agree as touching anything on this earth, it will be done of our Father who is in Heaven.

We believe that the ongoing operations of the synagogue of Satan and their global banking operations are not in line with your will. For your word says, 'Your kingdom come, Your will be done, on earth as it is in Heaven.' We know there are no criminal banks in Heaven. We have learned of the acts of wickedness the synagogue of Satan has perpetrated in the past, are perpetrating now and intend to continue perpetrating in the future. We therefore lift up the satanic banking families of the world in prayer now to be presented before You for judgement. We deem these malevolent families' operations to be unfit for the earth and therefore petition for the removal of their power from global economics completely. Father, let their wealth be confiscated and given to those who will regard the poor and disenfranchised. Let their media houses be exposed, put to shame and destroyed for covering up their operations from the public for all of these years. Father, let their banks be shut down and let honest governments print their own currency debt free.

Let God arise and the synagogue of Satan be scattered! Let their social, political and economic pillars be crushed and let their entire operations collapse in confusion and chaos. Father, let the Vatican altars be overthrown, crushed and scattered.

Let the marine kingdom industries be destroyed. Let fire crush their operations and let their wares be burned with fire. Let their laboratories be destroyed and let their biological, economic, and political weapons backfire on them, desecrate their garrisons and let them be utterly and totally defeated. Let the prison gates be opened and their prisoners be set free. Let financial chains of bondage be broken all over the world. Let the blinding light which Satan shines on the minds of men be overcome by the glorious light of the gospel. Father, let media platforms be taken over by Heaven's marketing team. Let Satan and his agents be exposed and embarrassed. Let there be billboards all over the earth advertising messages of love, hope and salvation. Let those in bondage to Freemasonry, seeking for a way out find salvation in Christ Jesus. Let there be programs and content on all media platforms including movies, series, commercials, documentaries, plays, godly music videos and more influence be given to the body of Christ. Let satanic propaganda be overwhelmed by the work of your Holy Spirit.

Finally Father, may true education replace false education and true media replace false media.

Let the satanic house of cards come tumbling down for it is written; Proverbs 14:11 "*The house of the wicked shall be overthrown: but the tabernacle of the upright shall flourish.*" Let the house of Rothschild be overthrown, let the memory of their name be forgotten from the face of the earth forever. May Satan's social, political and economic pillars be crushed and may the name of Jesus be glorified in eternal triumph forevermore. Bless the readers of this book with brilliant problem solving ideas, capital and resource management to be a blessing to their generation. May we finish well in Jesus name we pray, Amen!

If you have not made Jesus Christ the Lord of your life, and you know you're not born again, say this simple prayer and join the most beautiful family in existence. Just say;

"Oh God, I am a sinner, but I have heard Your word. I've made bad investments in life, and I would like to repent and give my life to Jesus and serve Him for the rest of my life. Please forgive me of my sins, make me a new creature. Write my name in the book of life and teach me to walk in your ways. In Jesus name I pray, amen."

If you prayed that prayer you are saved. I'd like to welcome you to the body of Christ! Join a bible teaching church. Not a Catholic Church, or a cult, but let the Holy Spirit lead you to a church where they teach the Bible, condemn sin, preach righteousness and speak often of the shed blood of Jesus. If they don't do those things, get out of there quick! Learn God's word, make that your number one priority. Without it, you're powerless and an easy target in this world.

And now, may the grace of our Lord Jesus Christ (Yeshua), the love of God (Yahweh) and the fellowship of the Holy Spirit, be with us all, now and forever more. Amen.

Printed in Great Britain
by Amazon

45226320R00156